Study Guide
to accompany

Sociology in a Changing World

FOURTH EDITION

WILLIAM KORNBLUM

and

CAROLYN D. SMITH

Harcourt Brace College Publishers
Fort Worth • Philadelphia • San Diego • New York • Orlando • Austin • San Antonio
Toronto • Montreal • London • Sydney • Tokyo

ISBN: 0-15-503292-5

Address for editorial correspondence:
Harcourt Brace College Publishers
301 Commerce Street, Suite 3700
Fort Worth, TX 76102

Address for orders:
Harcourt Brace &Company
6277 Sea Harbor Drive
Orlando, FL 32887

1-800-782-4479 or 1-800-433-0001 (in Florida)

Printed in the United States of America

7 8 9 0 1 2 3 4 5   066 10 9 8 7 6 5 4 3 2

Contents

Introduction

This Study Guide is designed to accompany *Sociology in a Changing World,* Fourth Edition, by William Kornblum. It can be used to review each chapter in the textbook or as a study aid in preparing for tests. Each chapter of the guide corresponds to a chapter of the textbook and is divided into the following sections:

- **Chapter Outline:** This brief outline will help you recall the main topics covered in the chapter.

- **Objectives:** Read the list of objectives and think about them before continuing your review. They will help you focus on the major concepts discussed in the chapter.

- **Review:** This section summarizes the material presented in the chapter, but key words are left out. Cover the answers with a sheet of paper, fill in the blanks, and then check your answers against the correct ones.

- **Matching Exercise:** Make sure you can match each term with its definition. (The answers are listed at the end of the study guide.) If you are not sure what is meant by a particular term, find it in the chapter (key terms are in bold type) and reread the section in which it appears.

- **Self-Test:** The self-test consists of fifteen multiple-choice and five true/false questions designed to test your comprehension of the material presented in the chapter. Again, the answers are listed at the end of the study guide. If any of your answers are incorrect, review the text pages indicated. At the end of the self-test are five short-answer questions designed to help you look at the subjects discussed in the chapter from a broader perspective—to compare and contrast different sociological perspectives, for example, or apply what you have learned to a real-world situation. These questions will give you some practice in answering essay questions.

Building Critical Thinking and Writing Skills

Good writing is a key to success in college. It can also be the secret of success in many occupations and professions such as law, science, and business. But what is good writing? And why is there so much emphasis on writing these days? The answer to the second question is easy: Along with the rapid expansion of the store of knowledge has come a growing need for people who can organize knowledge and write about it in ways that others will understand. But the first question is much harder to answer. There are many definitions of good writing, just as there are many kinds of writing. Here we will be dealing with several aspects of good writing, with emphasis on writing in the social sciences.

Perhaps the most important feature of strong writing is that it is clear and direct and comes to the point in every paragraph. In good writing, the author knows what he or she is trying to say in every sentence. To achieve this goal, one needs to be extremely critical of one's own ideas and the way they are organized, which is why critical thinking skills are so important to good writing. To be a good writer one must learn to ask critical questions about what one reads, to find weaknesses in arguments and expose fuzzy thinking—especially one's own.

Writing and Critical Thinking

In the social sciences we are constantly confronted with "received wisdoms"—ideas that people tend to believe without using their critical abilities to question them. Prejudices and commonsense assumptions about social life are among the received wisdoms that are especially damaging to efforts to think logically and scientifically about the social world. When one hears statements such as "There will always be some people who are selfish" or "It's human nature that causes crime" or "People on welfare just don't want to work," these are personal beliefs or prejudices that may or may not be accurate in the situation to which they are being applied. When stated repeatedly with no attempt to question their truth, they are the opposite of critical thought. And when used in sociological writing, they can lead to harsh criticism (and low grades).

But simple acceptance of received wisdoms is only one kind of uncritical thought. On a more sophisticated level, we find received wisdoms that serve as single explanations of social life. Extreme radicals, for example, may seek to explain all social problems as resulting from class conflict. Ultraconservatives, on the other hand, may explain social problems of all kinds as resulting from excess governmental interference. These are single ideas that one often hears used to explain situations that actually require more diverse and subtle explanations. Unless one is critical of such single explanations, one cannot write well about social life.

In thinking critically, it is helpful to ask a series of questions about any idea or statement: What is the point being made? Is that point supported by the facts? Can I think of instances in which it would not be justified? Does this point lead logically to other points in the argument in which it is presented? Does the point reflect a bias or prejudice or self-serving attitude on the part of its originator?

Written statements demand the same critical thought, no matter how famous their author is said to be. Written statements should also be subjected to a series of questions about the writing itself: Do the sentences make sense? Can they be simplified without doing harm to their meaning, and if so, why were they so long and complicated in the first place? On the other hand, are they too short and oversimplified? If so, does this mean that the writer has not given enough thought to the subject?

In a famous criticism of what he called Grand Theory, C. Wright Mills took aim at sociologists who write long, abstract passages of social theory. Here is an example of such a passage, followed by Mills's translation:

Harcourt Brace & Company.

Attachment to common values means, motivationally considered, that the actors have common "sentiments" in support of the value patterns, which may be treated as a "good thing" relatively independently of any specific instrumental "advantage" to be gained from such conformity, e.g., in the avoidance of negative sanctions. Furthermore, this attachment to common values, while it may fit the immediate gratificational needs of the actor, always has also a "moral" aspect in that to some degree this conformity defines the "responsibilities" of the actor in the wider, that is, social action systems in which he participates.

(from Talcott Parsons, The Social System)

When people share the same values, they tend to behave in accordance with the way they expect one another to behave. Moreover, they often treat such conformity as a very good thing—even when it seems to go against their immediate interests.

(Mills, 1959, p. 31)

By simplifying the dense writing in the first paragraph, Mills is trying to render it more intelligible to any reader. He is also trying to get to the points buried in the convoluted sentences so that their value can be assessed critically. This kind of critical thinking must be applied to ideas and statements, both those of others and one's own, if one is to write with strength and clarity.

Writing Assignments in Sociology Courses

Although the elements of good writing are the same no matter what the assignment, there are important differences in what one can be expected to produce in different kinds of writing assignments. Following are some suggestions for organizing and writing the most common types of written assignments in sociology courses: essay questions on exams, short themes, reading notes, and research papers.

Essay Questions. These are usually written in the student's handwriting in an exam booklet, known in many colleges and universities as a "blue book," under conditions of rather intense time pressure. These conditions tend to produce a good deal of anxiety, which is often reflected in poor-quality writing.

In fact, however, once a student has thought about what the instructor is looking for in a question, and about how to organize the answer, it is relatively easy to write a good essay. Here is a description of the process one might follow in answering an essay question like this one:

Distinguish between role conflict and role strain, giving examples of each. Why do you think role conflicts are more likely to occur in more complex societies than in simpler ones?

Before launching into the written answer, write an outline in schematic form. This outline will give you a structure and show the instructor what you were thinking about in preparing to write the answer. Try to stay with the outline as you do the actual writing. The more detailed and specific you have made the outline, the easier it will be to stay with it.

In the first paragraph or two of your answer, present the broadest idea needed to develop the essay. In our example, it would be a definition of what a role is and how it organizes important aspects of human behavior. Any time you define a term, using your own language or that of an authority, always try to offer an example that makes the definition concrete. Unless you show that you understand the concept of a role—that it is the behavior associated with a status in society—it will be difficult to go on to role conflict and role strain.

In the next section of the essay, write paragraphs that define role conflict and role strain. Again, be sure to provide examples. End this section with a brief paragraph that explains the difference between the two concepts. The last section of the essay must answer the second part of

Harcourt Brace & Company.

the question, which asks why role conflicts are more likely to appear in complex societies than in simpler ones. The answer deals with the greater number of roles that people in complex societies carry out; for example, a woman is typically a student, a mother, a worker, a committee member, and so on—a far greater number of roles than she would have in a traditional village society. The likelihood that these roles will demand behaviors that are incompatible, such as staying home with children and going to work in an office, is quite great. In a village society a woman is also a mother and a worker, but the roles are combined; her work in the fields is close by and her children are typically there with her, so the potential for conflict is less than it is when her roles require her to be in different places.

This was a rather simple essay to outline, especially since the major sections are suggested by the questions posed, which is not at all uncommon for essay exams. It is important to make sure you answer each of the questions and include a paragraph or section corresponding to each part of the overall essay question.

When you have finished writing your essay, *read it over and correct any obvious mistakes.* Essay questions in sociology are not typically judged on the basis of writing style or grammatical correctness, but you should get in the habit of always reading over what you have written. Take pride in your writing and polish it wherever possible. Corrections on an essay are acceptable; they show the instructor that you care. These are small touches that reveal a great deal about you as a student and future professional.

The Short Theme. This is usually a short piece of writing, about two or three pages, designed to test your ability to organize thoughts into a coherent argument or description. The question may be quite broad, such as "Describe how social change affects your own life." But such questions can usually be narrowed down. Social change involves changes occurring throughout society, but only those that impinge on your own life count in this assignment. Choose some examples and develop them into a coherent statement. Always use whole paragraphs and complete sentences.

Normally one begins academic writing assignments with an organizing paragraph that states the issue or theme and in three or four sentences explains how one will approach the problem or develop the theme. But it is always worthwhile to try for some innovation in the opening paragraph. A short vignette—that is, a brief story about how a specific change has altered your life or your immediate social world—would grab the reader's attention. From the vignette you can proceed to a more general statement of what the issues are, in this case how the events in the opening example are characteristic of larger-scale changes affecting others as well. This approach would make for an effective organizing strategy.

A short theme is an opportunity to try out some writing techniques, to be daring. But this does not mean that you need to labor long hours to construct "deep" thoughts or produce a smashing sentence. In fact, you should avoid sentences such as this one: "Social change affects my life in myriad ways, from the sublime to the ridiculous, from the mundane to the tragic, from the macro to the micro levels of my life." This is an example of what is often called "purple prose"; it is full of superficially impressive sounds and inflated claims but does not carry much meaning at all. What are the myriad ways? What social changes does the writer have in mind? This sentence sounds like a student trying out a mixture of sociological terms, such as *micro* and *macro levels,* and some literary ones, such as *tragedy* and *sublime.* A clearer sentence would be one such as this: "Social change affects every aspect of my life, from the most minor aspects of my behavior at home to the plans I have for the future." Then you would go on to explain what this sentence suggests by first dealing with the small-scale, micro-level changes and then describing the larger ones that affect your future. If you work your feelings into the writing through adjectives and statements about how you feel about the changes in your life, your essay will gain power without the need for any purple prose.

Reading Notes. These are often a precursor to a research paper. They demonstrate the kind of data or supporting material that you have been finding to use in the longer paper. Also, when students are involved in any professional field work for researchers they are often asked to prepare

Harcourt Brace & Company.

reading notes or to summarize literature. This assignment is therefore particularly useful in that it has direct applications to professional research and writing.

Reading notes must provide all the required bibliographic information at the top of the page where the entry begins. If you have never done a research bibliography or do not remember how to set down the information, consult a writer's manual such as the *Harbrace College Handbook* or *A Manual for Writers,* by Kate Turabian (published by the University of Chicago Press). Summarize what you have read and indicate whether it is a partial reading of a longer work by including the author's central problem or theme, the kinds of evidence he or she uses (for example, if it is an empirical study, make sure you briefly summarize what data were collected and when the original research was done; if it is a historical work, note the types of historical information included in the book, paper, and so on), and the conclusions or recommendations the author draws from the research. If you are looking for a specific argument or type of information and the reading does not have it, you should mention that as well. You can get a good idea about what goes into reading notes on research papers by consulting *Sociological Abstracts,* which provide up-to-date information about scholarly papers in all the subfields of sociology. For longer books you will want to write a note on each chapter or on the chapters that apply most directly to your project.

The Research Paper. This project is usually rather ambitious and may extend over an entire semester. An honors thesis may be a year-long project. The research papers one writes in college are a way of learning how to approach the research and writing one may do later when carrying out professional assignments—legal briefs, scientific papers, theses, prospectuses, and the like.

In the case of a one-semester research paper, it is a good idea to get started on the assignment as soon as possible. We all have had the experience of trying to "get over" at the end of a semester. It can be done, but usually with mediocre results and an unimpressive grade. You will be surprised to see how much you can accomplish with relative ease by the end of the semester if you follow a few simple guidelines: Choose a topic immediately, stick to it, and work on the project each week according to a planned schedule of *background research, brainstorming* and *note taking, thesis development* and *outlining, drafting,* and *rewriting.* Some of these phases can be undertaken simultaneously, but others clearly must await the completion of prior tasks.

Suppose, for example, that the topic of your sociology research paper is date rape, an issue about which a great deal of information is available in recent studies and articles, and one that raises larger issues of social criticism and social theory. First realize that you have a subject, or *topic,* not a thesis or argument or viewpoint. Date rape is a topic. The idea that the increase in reported incidents of date rape is explained by women's greater willingness to come forward about it is the beginning of a *thesis,* an argument that one could explore through research. It is important to move quickly from the broad topic of date rape to a more focused thesis. You may have strong feelings about the topic, and these can be helpful in framing your argument, but you must be careful that your own bias does not prevent you from learning from the research. It is not what you believed before doing the research that matters, but what you allow yourself to learn through the research itself.

Brainstorming is a process in which you think of as many ideas and issues that bear on the topic as possible. Sometimes it is worthwhile to brainstorm with friends, who will come up with other ideas and associations about the subject. The reading notes you prepare about articles and books on the subject will later serve as paragraphs or parts of paragraphs in your paper. But they can serve you well only if they are done well from the start. They should be legibly written or typed, with a few cogent quotations about important points that you may want to include in your paper.

The sources you use should represent solid contributions to the literature. For a sociology paper it is best to consult sociological journals and other sources. Start with *Sociological Abstracts,* the *American Journal of Sociology,* and *Society* magazine. Other sources will appear in the bibliographies of the articles you read. Finally, in gathering the sources for your paper be aware of what kinds of evidence best support the kind of argument you are making. If the issues are quantitative, involving increases or decreases in social phenomena, try to marshal at least some

Harcourt Brace & Company.

quantitative indicators of what it is you are studying or trying to show. Numerical tables or graphs can be extremely valuable in such presentations.

For a more theoretical argument you will need to present the ideas of many different commentators and theorists. In that case it is important to know how to use quotations, to be careful in selecting the best and most succinct ones, and to know how to paraphrase ideas in your own words. Make sure that whenever you are using other people's words you cite the source, including the page on which the quoted material appears. Even when you are using an idea from another source or a fact stated in your own words, try to show what sources you used to make the statement. Always do so. Failure to document can lead you into plagiarism. To cite carefully is to demonstrate how much research you have done.

In constructing the outline for your first draft, put a good deal of thought into what the major sections of the paper will be and how they will be titled. Try to use section titles that convey meaning and help the reader know what you are saying in the section. For example, a beginning section titled "Introduction" is not very helpful. A title such as "The Date Rape Controversy: An Overview" is somewhat longer and carries valuable information. It is extremely useful to provide a brief summary paragraph at the end of each section of the paper, ending with a transition that will prepare the reader for what is coming next. For example: "This introduction has presented the basic terms of the debate over this growing social problem. The scholarly literature on the subject offers additional insight into the recent research on the scope and explanations of date rape." This transition clearly indicates that the next section of the paper will discuss issues that you have identified in your literature review.

"Say what you are going to do, do it, and say what you have done." So goes an old rule of essay and term paper organization. This rule is mainly a caution not to hold your best ideas, findings, or recommendations until the end of the paper because your fickle reader may never get there. Put your main points or findings in the introduction and spend the remainder of the paper elaborating on them. End by summarizing why they are your main points, and you will have a solid conceptual base for your facts and ideas.

The Writing Process

Before You Start. Perhaps the most important part of the writing process is the thinking you do before actually starting to write. If you have a clear idea about what you want to say and why, it will come across in your writing. This pre-writing stage can be broken down into a series of steps, as follows:

1. Be sure you understand exactly what you are expected to do. Read the instructions carefully, and then read them again. If you are unsure about something, *ask*. For exams, be sure you understand whether you are to answer all the essay questions listed or choose one or two of them. For term papers, be sure you understand what is expected in terms of length, treatment of bibliographic material, and the like.
2. Be sure you know exactly what you are going to write about. If you are choosing a topic, try to choose one that you are interested in and about which you know something. Make sure it is not so broad that you could write a book about it; set limits on the topic. Think about what you really want to write about—the thesis—and then state it in a sentence. In the case of date rape, you could write about how date rape is covered by the media, about trends in the reporting of incidents of date rape, about feminist views on the subject, and so on. Each of these could be the subject of a long paper. If you were to write about the reporting of incidents of date rape, your thesis statement might be, "The number of reported incidents of date rape has been increasing because women are more willing to talk about their experience."
3. Make a rough list of the aspects of the topic about which you will be writing. Just jot them down; do not worry about organizing them. Making lists is especially important when

Harcourt Brace & Company.

answering essay questions on exams. If you have to list items in the margin of the test paper, go ahead. This step is too important to be skipped.

4. Think about the items on your list. How do they relate to one another? Which ones should be discussed first so that the later ones make more sense? Is there an obvious order in which they should be discussed, such as chronological order? Rearrange the items in a logical order before you start writing.

5. (This step applies to longer assignments.) Make an outline based on your list, and as you think of additional points to be made, work them into the outline. The outline does not have to be a formal document with roman numerals, capital letters, and so on. It just has to make clear which items are the main points and which items are supporting arguments and examples. Do not start writing until you have organized and outlined the material you are going to cover. Outlining may seem like a waste of time, and it is often avoided even by professional writers. But it is an essential skill. With a good outline, a paper or report will practically write itself. On the other hand, when material is not organized beforehand, the writing process is likely to be laborious and time consuming.

The First Draft. In writing your first draft, pay special attention to the introduction. It is the most important part of your essay or paper; it sets forth your argument and gets the reader's attention. Throughout the paper, follow your outline even if you are tempted to depart from it. Going off on tangents will take up valuable time and weaken your argument.

At this stage it is important to let your ideas flow even if your sentences sound a bit awkward and you are not sure exactly which words to use. Matters of style and usage can be dealt with when you revise your draft. Keep in mind, however, that no amount of revision will turn a sloppy, poorly thought out paper into a good one. At any stage of the writing process you should avoid pretentious and meaningless phrasing and wordiness. As the noted essayist George Orwell put it, "Words like *phenomenon, element, individual* (as noun), *objective, categorical, effective, virtual, basic, primary, promote, constitute, exhibit, exploit, utilize, eliminate, liquidate,* are used to dress up simple statements and give an air of scientific impartiality to biased judgments." Orwell illustrates his point with the following example, using a well-known verse from *Ecclesiastes:*

> I returned and saw under the sun, that the race is not to the swift, nor the battle to the strong, neither yet bread to the wise, nor yet riches to men of understanding, nor yet favour to men of skill; but time and chance happeneth to them all.

Here is the same verse, rewritten by Orwell in clumsy, pretentious prose:

> Objective consideration of contemporary phenomena compels the conclusion that success or failure in competitive activities exhibits no tendency to be commensurate with innate capacity, but that a considerable element of the unpredictable must invariably be taken into account.

(1949, p. 360)

Revising. Peg Bracken, author of the *I Hate to Cook Book,* has this to say about leftovers: "When in doubt, throw it out." The same could be said about revising. Do not become wedded to your words—sometimes your most useful tool is the wastebasket.

It is important to be tough on yourself when you revise. If a sentence does not say what you want it to say, rewrite it or write a new one. If a word is not quite right, use another one. If your paragraphs are too long, shorten them. Rarely will the original version be better than the revised one.

Revision is an essential part of the writing process. Do not skip it—bite the bullet and *do* it! (Actually, do it two or three times.) Revise your introductory paragraphs last—they are the most important part of the paper because they are intended to get the reader's attention. Try putting yourself in the reader's shoes and read your opening paragraphs. Do they state the subject clearly? Will they grab the reader's attention? If not, rewrite them.

Harcourt Brace & Company.

The process of writing, revising, and preparing the final version is much easier if it is done on a computer using a word-processing program.

Preparing the Final Version. When you are satisfied with what you have written, you are ready to prepare the final version of the paper. Before you do so, check your spelling and punctuation. You can use a spell-checker program, but you must proofread the material yourself as well; the spell checker will not catch certain kinds of errors. It is a good idea to add a table of contents listing the main sections of the paper, and be sure to include a bibliography in the style required by your instructor.

The final version of the paper should be double spaced, with one-inch margins, on 8-1/2" X 11" plain bond paper.

Improving Your Writing Style

If you feel confident that you have said what you want to say but believe that you could say it better, you are concerned about your writing style. It is not difficult to improve your style if you consider some of the suggestions and guidelines provided by experts in the field. Among the best-known books on this subject is *The Elements of Style,* by William Strunk and E. B. White. We strongly recommend that you purchase a copy of this refreshingly short book; it is almost certainly available in your college bookstore.

Strunk and White provide the following guidelines for developing a good writing style:

1. Put yourself in the background.
2. Write in a way that comes naturally.
3. Write with nouns and verbs.
4. Do not overstate.
5. Avoid the use of qualifiers (*very, somewhat,* and so on).
6. Do not affect a breezy manner.
7. Use orthodox spelling. (Avoid spellings such as *nite* and *thru.*)
8. Do not explain too much.
9. Do not construct awkward adverbs (*tangledly, tiredly,* and so on).
10. Make sure the reader knows who is speaking.
11. Do not inject opinion.
12. Use figures of speech sparingly.
13. Do not take shortcuts at the cost of clarity.
14. Avoid foreign languages. (Readers will not be impressed by phrases such as "a certain *je ne sais quoi.*")
15. Prefer the standard to the offbeat.

George Orwell has written eloquently on this subject as well. He has this to say about style:

> When you think of a concrete object, you think wordlessly, and then, if you want to describe the thing you have been visualizing you probably hunt about till you find the exact words that seem to fit it. When you think of something abstract you are more inclined to use words from the start, and unless you make a conscious effort to prevent it, the existing dialect will come rushing in and do the job for you, at the expense of blurring or even changing your meaning. Probably it is better to put off using words as long as possible and get one's meaning as clear as one can through pictures or sensations. Afterward one can choose—not simply *accept*—the phrases that will best cover the meaning, and then switch round and decide what impression one's words are likely to make on another person. This last effort of the mind cuts out all stale or mixed images, all prefabricated phrases, needless repetitions, and humbug and vagueness generally. But one can often be in doubt about the effect of a word or a phrase, and one needs rules that one can rely on when instinct fails. I think the following rules will cover most cases:

Harcourt Brace & Company.

(i)   Never use a metaphor, simile, or other figure of speech which you are used to seeing in print.

(ii)   Never use a long word where a short one will do.

(iii)   If it is possible to cut a word out, always cut it out.

(iv)   Never use the passive where you can use the active.

(v)   Never use a foreign phrase, a scientific word, or a jargon word if you can think of an everyday English equivalent.

(vi)   Break any of these rules sooner than say anything outright barbarous.

(1949, pp. 365–366)

Avoiding Sexist Language

It is essential to avoid sexist language in your writing, but you also want to avoid twisting the language or writing in an unnatural fashion. A few basic rules can help you avoid both extremes:

1. Keep in mind that occupation or profession is independent of sex. Do not imply that all homemakers or secretaries are women or that all managers or professors are men.

2. When using a pronoun to refer to an antecedent who could be of either sex, such as "the teacher," use *he or she, him or her, his or her.* Or use the plural—"teachers . . . they . . . "

3. Avoid nouns ending in *-man* unless they apply to an identified male. Words such as *head* or *chair* can be used instead of *chairman, police officer* instead of *policeman, letter carrier* instead of *mailman.*

4. Use *humanity* rather than *mankind* in referring to the human race.

Avoiding Common Mistakes

Certain errors of spelling and usage crop up in many people's writing. Some words are frequently misused because they are confused with words they resemble. Others are considered unsuitable in formal writing; they include informal words and phrases (colloquialisms) and slang. There are also certain expressions that are considered nonstandard and should be avoided. The following list presents some of the most frequently misused words and expressions.

a, an. Use *a* before a word beginning with a consonant sound: *a* car, *a* hat, *a* history test, *a* *u*nion (*u* pronounced as if preceded by consonant *y*).

Use *an* before a word beginning with a vowel sound: *an* accident, *an* image, *an* honest person, (*h* is silent), *an* uncle.

accept, except. *Accept* (verb) means "to receive": She *accepted* the gift.

Except (usually preposition) means "excluding": Everyone clapped *except* Farley.

Note: *Except* is occasionally a verb, meaning "to exclude": If you *except* the fifth clause, the rule applies in her case.

actual fact. See *fact.*

adapt, adopt. *Adapt* means "to adjust or make suitable." It is usually followed by *to: He adapted to* his new social environment.

Adopt means "to take as one's own": He *adopted* the habits of his new social environment. They *adopted* a child.

advice, advise. *Advice* (noun) means "counsel": Take my *advice.*

Advise (verb) means "to give advice": I *advise* you to go.

affect, effect. Most commonly, *affect* (verb) means "to influence": The war *affected* everyone.

Most commonly, *effect* (noun) means "a result": One *effect* of the war was mass starvation.

Note: Less commonly, *affect* (as a verb) means "to pretend or imitate": He *affected* a British accent. *Effect* (as a verb) means "to accomplish, to bring about": The medicine effected a cure.

Harcourt Brace & Company.

aggravate. Colloquial when used for *irritate* or *annoy*: The children *annoyed* (not *aggravated*) him.

aisle, isle. An *aisle* is a passage between rows of seats. An *isle* is an island.

all, all of. *All of* is redundant when used with common nouns: *All* (not *all of*) the men arrived on time.

allusion, illusion, delusion. *Allusion* means "an indirect reference": Her Biblical *allusions* drew praise.
Illusion means "a false perception eventually recognized as false": It was an optical *illusion*.
Delusion refers to a false perception or belief that is held as a result of self-deception: He labored under the *delusion* that everyone admired him.

almost. See *most*.

a lot, alot, allot. *A lot* is colloquial when used for *many* or *much*: He had *many* (not *a lot of*) relatives. He was *much* (not *a lot*) better. Avoid the misspelling *alot*.
Allot means "to apportion or give by some plan": The officials will *allot* each large family a subsidy.

already, all ready. Use *all ready* (meaning "completely ready") wherever *ready* alone makes sense: The squad was *all ready*. (The squad was *ready*.)
Elsewhere, use *already* (meaning "previously" or "by this time"): She had *already* eaten. He is here *already*.

alright. Incorrect for *all right*.

altogether, all together. Use *all together* (meaning "in a group") wherever *together* alone makes sense: We were *all together* at the party. (We were *together* at the party.)
Elsewhere use *altogether* (meaning "wholly, completely, in all"): Custer was *altogether* surprised at Little Big Horn.

alumna, alumnus. An *alumna* is a female former student of a school or college. The plural is *alumnae* (usually pronounced with a final sound of *EE*).
An *alumnus* is the male or mixed-gender equivalent; the plural is *alumni* (usually pronounced with the final sound of *EYE*).

always. Do not contradict *always* (meaning "all the time") by adding *generally* or *usually* (meaning "most of the time") as a modifier.
Wrong: She *generally* (or *usually*) *always* wins.
Right: She *always* (or *usually* or *generally*) wins.

among. See *between*.

amoral, immoral. *Amoral* means "not concerned with morality": An infant's acts are *amoral*.
Immoral means "against morality": Murder is *immoral*.

amount, number. *Amount* refers to things in bulk or mass: a large *amount* of grain; no *amount* of persuasion.
Number refers to countable objects: a *number* of apples.

and etc. See *etc.*

and/or. Avoid it except in legal and business writing:
Weak: Linda plans to get a degree in psychology *and/or* education.
Better: Linda plans to get a degree in psychology, education, or both.

angry at, about, with. One becomes *angry at* or *about* a thing but *angry with* a person. See also *mad*.

ante-, anti-. Both are prefixes. *Ante-* means "before": *anteroom, antedate*.
Anti- means "against": *antibody, antisocial*.

anxious, eager. *Anxious* conveys worry or unease: She is *anxious* about her safety.
Eager conveys strong desire: He is *eager* to eat.

anymore, any more. *Any more* means "additional": Are there *any more* noodles?
Anymore means "at present": You don't call *anymore*.

anyone, any one. *Anyone* means "any person": Has *anyone* here seen Kelly?
Any one refers to any single item of a number of items: If you like my drawings, take *any one* you wish.

Harcourt Brace & Company.

anyone, everyone, someone, anybody, everybody, somebody. Use a singular verb and pronoun with these words.

anyplace, everyplace, noplace, someplace. Colloquial. Precise writers and speakers prefer *anywhere, everywhere, nowhere, somewhere.*

anyways. Nonstandard; use *anyway* or *any way.*

anywheres, everywheres, nowheres, somewheres. Nonstandard; use *anywhere, everywhere,* and so on.

apt, likely, liable. *Apt* is used when probability is based on normal, habitual, or customary tendency: She is *apt* to blush when embarrassed.
Likely indicates mere probability: It is *likely* to rain tomorrow.
Liable indicates an undesirable or undesired risk: He's *liable* to harm himself by playing with a loaded gun.

aren't I. Obviously ungrammatical (*are I not*), though some authorities accept it in informal use. *Am I not* is the alternative.

as, because, since. To express cause, make *because* your first choice; it is most precise.
As and *since* may be ambiguous, conveying either a time or cause relation: *Since* you left, I've been sick.
Since is acceptable informally when there is no ambiguity. *As* is the least acceptable.

as, like. See *like.*

at. Redundant with *where*: *Where* is she? (not *Where* is she at?)

aural. See verbal.

awful, awfully. *Awful* is colloquial when used adverbially to mean "very bad, ugly, shocking": His language was *shocking* (not *awful*).
Awful is incorrect when used adverbially to mean "very": That pizza was *very* (not *awful*) good.
Awfully is colloquial when used to mean "very": Jan is *very* (not *awfully*) happy.

awhile. Do not use the adverb *awhile* after *for.* One may stay *awhile* (adverb), stay a *while* (noun), stay for a *while* (noun), but not for *awhile* (adverb).

bad, badly. *Badly* (adverb) is colloquial when used for *very much* or *greatly* or after a linking verb (*be, seem,* and so on): She wanted *very much* (not *badly*) to be there.
Bad (adjective) correctly follows a linking verb: I feel *bad.*

because. See *reason is because* and *as, because, since.*

being as (how), being that. Colloquial or nonstandard for *as, because,* or *since* (which see).

beside, besides. *Beside* (preposition) means "by the side of": A man was sitting *beside* me (in the seat next to mine).
Besides (preposition) means "in addition to" or "except": Only one man was sitting *besides* me (everyone else was standing). As a conjunctive adverb, it means "in addition": He is ugly; *besides,* he is boorish.

better, had better. Always add *had* or its contraction, *'d,* before *better* when you mean *should* or *ought to*:
Wrong: You *better* milk the cows.
Right: You *had* (or You*'d*) better milk the cows.

between. A preposition; the objective case must follow it: *between* you and *me,* not *between* you and *I.*

between, among. *Between* implies *two* persons or things in a relationship; *among* implies *three* or *more*; Must I decide *between* cake and ice cream? The estate was divided *among* the five children.

born, borne. For all meanings of *bear* except "give birth," the past participle is *borne. Borne* is correct in this sense also when it follows *have* or precedes *by*: Mrs. Jackson had already *borne* six children. The half-sisters were *borne* by different mothers.
Born is the correct past participle in other contexts relating to birth: The child was *born* in Brazil.

Harcourt Brace & Company.

brake, break. *Brake* refers to stopping: Apply the *brake*. *Brake* the car carefully.
Break refers to destroying, damaging, exceeding, or interrupting: Don't *break* the glass. I'll *break* the record. Take a ten-minute *break*.

bring, take. Precise usage requires *bring* when you mean "to come (here) with" and *take* when you mean "to go (there) with."

bunch. Colloquial when meaning "crowd; group of people." Say "a *bunch* of bananas" but not "a *bunch* of friends."

bust, busted, bursted. Incorrect forms of the verb *burst*, of which the three principal parts are *burst, burst, burst*: Yesterday the water pipes *burst* (or *had burst*).

but that, but what. Colloquial for *that*: I don't doubt *that* (not *but that*) he'll come.

but yet. Redundant; use either: old *but* good; old *yet* good.

can, may. *Can* means "to be able": *Can* he lift the log? *May* means "to have permission": *May* I go with you?

can't hardly, can't scarcely. A double negative. Say "I *can't* hear her" or "I *can hardly* (or *can scarcely*) hear her."

can't help but. Colloquial for *can't help*:
Colloquial: I *can't help but* admire him.
Formal: I *can't help* admiring him.

canvas, canvass. A *canvas* is a cloth: Buy a *canvas* tent.
Canvass means "to solicit": *Canvass* the area for votes.

capital, capitol. Use *capitol* for the building where a legislature meets: The senator posed on the steps of the state *capitol*.
Elsewhere, use *capital*: Albany is the state *capital* (chief city). The firm has little *capital* (money). It was a *capital* (first rate) idea. The defendant has committed a *capital* offense (one punishable by death).

carat, caret, carrot. Gold and gems are weighed in *carats*. A *caret* (^) signals an omission: I ^ going home. A *carrot* is a vegetable: Eat your *carrots*.

casual, causal. *Casual* means "occurring by chance, informal, unplanned": *causal* means "involving cause."

censor, censure. To *censor* is to examine written, filmed, or broadcast material to delete objectionable content: How dare you *censor* my article!
To *censure* is to criticize or blame: The officer was *censured* for misconduct.

cite, site, sight. *Cite* means "quote an authority or give an example": He will *cite* Shakespeare's sonnet about age.
Site means "location": Here is the new building *site*.
Sight refers to seeing: His *sight* was failing. They have *sighted* the enemy.

classic, classical. *Classic* means "of the highest class or quality": *War and Peace* is a *classic* novel.
Classical means "pertaining to the art and life of ancient Greece and Rome": Mae is in Greece studying *classical* art. *Classical* music refers to symphonies, opera, and the like.

coarse, course. *Coarse* means "rough, not fine": *coarse* wool.
A *course* is a path or a series of lessons: race *course*, art *course*.

compare to, compare with. *Compare to* means "to point out one or more similarities": Sports writers are *comparing* the rookie *to* Hank Aaron.
Compare with means "to examine in order to find similarities and differences": Have you ever *compared* the new Ford *with* the Plymouth?

compliment, complement. *Compliment* means "to express praise": He *complimented* Beatrice on her good taste.
Complement means "to complete, enhance, or bring to perfection": The illustrations should *complement* the text.
The nouns *compliment* and *complement* are distinguished similarly.

Harcourt Brace & Company.

comprise, compose, include. *Comprise* means "to be made up of (in entirety)": New York City *comprises* five boroughs.

Compose means the opposite, "to make up": Five boroughs *compose* New York City.

Include means "to contain (but not necessarily in entirety)": New York City *includes* the boroughs of Brooklyn and Queens.

connect up. See *up*.

consensus. Avoid the trite and redundant *consensus of opinion*. Use *consensus* alone ("general agreement").

contact. *Contact* as a verb meaning "to get in touch with" is still not acceptable in formal writing. *Contact* as a noun meaning "source" has become accepted.

continual, continuous. *Continual* means "frequently repeated": He worked in spite of continual interruptions.

Continuous means "without interruption": We heard the *continuous* roar of the falls.

continued on. Often redundant; omit *on*: We *continued* (not *continued on*) our journey. But: We *continued on* Highway 280.

convince, persuade. *Convince* emphasizes changing a person's belief: *Convince* me of your sincerity.

Persuade emphasizes moving a person to action: The officer's speech *persuaded* Pat to enlist.

correspond to, correspond with. *Correspond to* means "to be similar or analogous to": Our Congress *corresponds to* the British Parliament.

Correspond with also means "to communicate with through exchange of letters."

could of, might of, ought to of, should of, would of. All wrong; *of* results from mishearing the contraction *'ve* (*have*). Write *could have, would have,* and so on.

council, counsel, consul. *Council* means "a deliberative assembly of persons": The city *council* convenes at noon.

Counsel (noun) means "advice" or "attorney": He gave me good *counsel* when he told me to stop procrastinating. The *counsel* for the defense filed an appeal.

Counsel (verb) means "to give advice": He will *counsel* me about postgraduate plans.

Consul means "an officer in the foreign service": The distinguished guest was the *consul* from Spain.

credible, credulous, creditable. *Credible* means "believable": A good witness should be *credible*.

Credulous means "too ready to believe; gullible": A *credulous* person is easily duped.

Creditable means "praiseworthy": The young pianist gave a *creditable* performance of a difficult work.

data, phenomena, strata, media. These are plural forms: Those *data* are available. The singular forms are *datum* (rarely used), *phenomenon, stratum, medium*.

Note: *Data* is gaining acceptance also as a singular when it refers to a single mass of information: All your *data* has been lost.

decent, descent. *Decent* means "proper, right": It's the *decent* thing to do.

Descent means "a going down" or "ancestry": The *descent* was steep. She's of Welsh *descent*.

delusion. See *allusion*.

device, devise. A *device* (noun) is an invention or a piece of equipment: I made this *device*.

To *devise* (verb) is to invent: *Devise* a new mousetrap.

different from, different than. Formal usage requires *different from*: Her dress is *different from* yours. The tendency is growing, however, to accept *different than* when a clause follows, since it seems simpler: His response was *different than* (rather than *different from what*) I expected.

differ from, differ with. *Differ from* expresses unlikeness: This book *differs from* the others in giving more details.

Differ with expresses divergence of opinion: I *differ with* you about the importance of the tax bill.

Harcourt Brace & Company.

discuss, discus, disgust. To *discuss* is to talk: Let's *discuss* the election.

A *discus* is a disc-shaped object: Throw the *discus.*

Disgust refers to being offensive: War *disgusts* me.

disinterested, uninterested. *Uninterested* means simply "not interested": Pat is *uninterested* in mechanics.

Disinterested means "not influenced by personal interest; impartial, unbiased": Only a truly *disinterested* person should serve as an arbitrator.

dived, dove. *Dived* is the preferred past tense and past participle of *dive*: The youngsters *dived* (not *dove*) for coins.

due (to). *Due to* is in common use as a preposition. However, strict usage requires *because of*: We were late *because of* (not *due to*) traffic.

Due to is correct as an adjective following a linking verb: Our lateness was *due to* traffic. See also *fact that.*

each and every. Redundant; use either: "*each* of us," "*every* one of us," but not "*each and every* one of us."

each other, one another. *Each other* refers to *two* persons or things, *one another* refers to *three or more.*

eager. See *anxious.*

effect. See *affect.*

elicit, illicit. To *elicit* is to draw forth: *Elicit* some response. *Illicit* means "illegal": Shun *illicit* drugs.

emigrate, immigrate. *Emigrate* means "to leave a country"; *immigrate* means "to enter a new country": Millions *emigrated* from Europe. They *immigrated* to America.

eminent, imminent. *Eminent* means "distinguished": She's an *eminent* surgeon.

Imminent means "about to happen": Rain is *imminent.*

end up. See *up.*

ensure, insure. Use *insure* when referring to insurance (protection against loss): You should *insure* your house.

Ensure is often preferred for "make sure, make safe": These tires will *ensure* that you'll never skid.

enthuse. Colloquial for *become enthusiastic*: She *becomes enthusiastic* (not *enthuses*) about everything.

envelop, envelope. To *envelop* is to surround: Fog *envelops* us.

An *envelope* holds a letter: Seal the *envelope.*

etc. Avoid *etc.* (meaning "and others") in formal paragraph writing. Use *and others* or *and so forth.* Better, rephrase the sentence to avoid all of these:

Weak: Jill prefers reading Twain, Howells, *and so forth.*

Better: Jill prefers writers *such as* Twain and Howells.

Always avoid *and etc.*; it is redundant.

everybody. See *anyone.*

everyone, every one. Use *everyone* where you can substitute *everybody*: *Everyone* (*everybody*) wishes you well. Elsewhere, use *every one* (usually followed by *of*): *Every one* of the roses died. See also *anyone.*

everyplace, everywheres. See *anyplace, anywheres.*

every so often. Colloquial for *occasionally.* Also colloquial: *every which way, every bit as, every once in a while.*

except. See *accept.*

fact. *Actual fact, real fact,* and *true fact* are usually redundant.

fact that. Wordy. For *due to the fact that,* say *because*; for *except for the fact that,* say *except that*; or recast the sentence:

Wordy: *Due to the fact that he was late,* we lost.

Concise: We lost *because he was late.*

Wordy: *The fact that he was late* made us lose.

Concise: *His lateness* made us lose.

Harcourt Brace & Company.

famous, notable, notorious. *Famous* means "widely known"; it usually has favorable connotations.

Notable means "worthy of note" or "prominent"; a person can be *notable* without being *famous*.

Notorious means "widely known in an unfavorable way": Bluebeard was *notorious* for being a bad husband.

farther, further. *Farther* refers to distance: He walked *farther* than I did.

Further means "to a greater extent or degree": Let's discuss the matter *further*.

fewer, less. Use *fewer* with countable things; *fewer* refers to number: She has *fewer* assets than I have.

Use *less* with things that are not countable but are considered in bulk or mass; *less* refers to quantity: She has *less* wealth than I have.

fine. The adjective *fine* is much overused as a vague word of approval, as "a *fine* boy." Use a more precise word. As an adverb meaning "well" ("He does *fine*"), it is colloquial. *Fine* also means "subtle" or "not coarse."

folks. Colloquial for *family, relatives, people.*

formally, formerly. *Formally* means "according to proper form": Introduce us *formally*.

Formerly means "previously": They *formerly* lived here.

former, first; latter, last. *Former* and *latter* refer to the first and second named of two; *first* and *last* refer to items in a series.

forth, fourth. *Forth* means "forward": Go *forth* and conquer.

Fourth is 4th: I was *fourth* in line.

funny. Do not use in formal writing to mean "odd" or "peculiar."

generally always. See *always*.

good. Do not use this adjective for the adverb *well*: The car runs *well* (not *good*).

As an adjective, *good* may correctly follow a linking verb: She feels *good* about winning.

got. See *have got*.

had of. Incorrect for *had*: I wish I *had* (or *I'd*—not *I had of* or *I'd of*) seen the show.

had ought. Incorrect for *ought*: I *ought* (not *had ought*) to go.

Hadn't ought is also incorrect. Use *ought not*.

half. Say *a half* or *half a(n),* not *a half a(n)*: Fill a *half* page (or *half a* page, but not *a half a* page).

hanged, hung. *Hanged* means "executed": Judas *hanged* himself.

Hung means "suspended": The picture was *hung*.

hardly. See *can't hardly*.

have got. Colloquial for *have:* I *have* (not *have got*) a dollar.

healthy, healthful. *Healthy* means "possessing health": The children are *healthy*.

Healthful means "conducive to health": Good food is *healthful*.

help. See *can't help but*.

herself, himself, myself, yourself. Do not substitute these intensive pronouns for the personal pronouns *I, you, him, her*: Grace and *you* (not *yourself*) are invited. She sent tickets to Don and *me* (not *myself*).

hisself. Incorrect for *himself*. He blames *himself* (not *hisself*) for the accident.

historic, historical. Strictly, *historic* means "famous or important in history": July 4, 1776, is a *historic* date.

Historical means "pertaining to history": Verna reads *historical* novels.

hopefully. Strictly, it means "full of hope": Christy *hopefully* awaited the posting of grades. In formal use, avoid it in the sense of "it is hoped that": *We hope that* (not *Hopefully*) the train will arrive on time.

how. See *being as (how), seeing as how*.

if, whether. *If* can be unclear when used to introduce alternative conditions. "Tell us *if* you see him" can mean not only "Tell us *whether* (or not) you see him" but also "*In case* you ever see him, tell us." Use *whether* for clarity.

illicit. See *elicit*.

Harcourt Brace & Company.

illusion. See *allusion.*

immigrate. See *emigrate.*

imminent. See *eminent.*

immoral. See *amoral.*

imply, infer. The writer or speaker *implies*; the reader or listener *infers.*
> *Imply* means "to state indirectly or suggest": He *implied* that we were at fault.
> *Infer* means "to draw a conclusion or derive by reasoning": I *inferred* from his statement that he blamed us.

in, into. *Into* indicates movement from outside to inside: Fido ran *into* the house.
> Otherwise, use *in*: Fido stays *in* the house at night.

in back of. Colloquial for *behind, at the back of, back of.*

include. See *comprise.*

incredible, incredulous. A fact or happening is *incredible* (unbelievable): Her thirty-foot putt was *incredible.*
> A person is *incredulous* (unbelieving): He was *incredulous* when told of her thirty-foot putt.

individual, person, party. Do not use *party* or *individual* when you mean simply *person*: A *person* (not an *individual* or a *party*) that I met told me the news.
> Except in legal and telephone-company language, and when you mean "one taking part," do not use *party* to refer to one person.
> Use *individual* only when emphasizing a person's singleness: Will you act with the group or as an *individual*?

ingenious, ingenuous. *Ingenious* means "clever"; *ingenuous* means "naive, frank."

in regards to. Incorrect for *in regard to*, or *as regards.*

inside of. Often redundant; omit *of* or use *within*: He was *inside* (not *inside of*) the room.
> *Inside of* is colloquial when used in reference to time or distance: I shall come *within* (not *inside of*) an hour. I was *within* (not *inside of*) a mile of my destination.
> "The *inside* of the house" is correct; here, *inside* is a noun.

instance, instant, instant's. *Instance* means "a case or example": He cited an *instance* of discrimination.
> *Instant* (noun) means "a brief time, a particular point in time, a moment": Come here this *instant*!
> *Instant* (adjective) means "urgent or immediate": An *instant* need is food for the poor. Do you like *instant* coffee?
> *Instant's* is the possessive form of the noun *instant*: He came at an *instant's* notice.

insure. See *ensure.*

irregardless. There is no such word. Use *regardless.*

irrelevant. This word means "not related to the point or subject." Notice the letters *rel* as in *related.* There is no such word as *irrevelant.*

isle. See *aisle.*

is when, is where. Avoid both expressions except when referring to a time or place:
> Wrong: A treaty *is when* nations sign an agreement.
> Right: A treaty *is* a signed agreement among nations.
> Right: Home *is where* the heart is. (place)

it being. An awkward substitute for *since it is.*

its, it's. *Its* is the possessive of *it*: The dog wagged *its* tail.
> *It's* is the contraction of *it is.* Use *it's* only if you can correctly substitute *it is* in your sentence: *It's* (*It is*) the best thing.

kid, kids. Colloquial for *child, children.*

kind of, sort of. Colloquial if used for *somewhat* or *rather.*

kind of a, sort of a. Omit the *a.* He wanted *some kind of* (not *some kind of a)* book.

last, latter. See *former.*

Harcourt Brace & Company.

later, latter. *Later,* the comparative form of *late,* means "more late."
Latter refers to the second of two things mentioned. If more than two are mentioned, use *last* instead of *latter.*

lay. See *lie.*

lead, led. *Lead* (rhymes with *need*) is the present tense of the verb meaning "to conduct, to go at the head of, to show the way": She can *lead* us to safety.
Led is the past tense and past participle of the same verb: She *led* us to safety. She has *led* us to safety.
Lead (rhymes with *dead*) is a metal: I need a *lead* pipe.

learn, teach. *Learn* means "to acquire knowledge": We *learned* irregular verbs.
Teach means "to impart knowledge": The professor *taught* us irregular verbs.

leave, let. *Leave* means "to depart": I must *leave* now.
Let means "to permit": *Let* me go.

less. See *fewer.*

lessen, lesson. To *lessen* is to diminish: His pain *lessened.*
A *lesson* is a unit of learning: Study your *lesson.*

liable, likely. See *apt.*

lie, lay. *Lie* means "to rest" and is an intransitive verb (it never takes an object): He makes me *lie* down in green pastures. The islands *lie* under the tropical sun. Here *lies* Jeremiah Todd.
Lay means "to put, to place," and is a transitive verb (it must take an object): *lay* your *head* on this pillow. Let me *lay* your fears to rest.
To complicate matters, the past tense of *lie* is spelled and pronounced the same as the present tense of *lay*:

Present	Past	Past Participle
lie (rest)	lay (rested)	(has) lain (rested)
lay (place)	laid (placed)	(has) laid (placed)

Yesterday Sandra *lay* (rested) too long in the sun. She should not have *lain* (rested) there so long. Yesterday the workers *laid* (placed) the foundation. They have *laid* (placed) it well.

like, as. In formal English, do not use *like* (preposition) where *as* or *as if* (conjunction) sounds right: He looks *as if* (not *like*) he's angry. She died just *as* (not *like*) her mother did.

loose, lose. *Loose* (usually adjective—rhymes with *goose*) is the opposite of *tight* or *confined*: A *loose* coupling caused the wreck. The lions are *loose*!
Loose is also sometimes a verb: *Loose* my bonds.
Lose (verb—rhymes with *news*) is the opposite of *to find* or *win*: Did you *lose* your wallet? We may *lose* the game.

lots, lots of. Colloquial if used for *much* or *many.*

mad, angry. In formal English, do not use *mad* to mean "angry." The common formal meaning of *mad* is "insane" or "insanely foolish": Do not be *angry* with me (not *mad* at me).

marvelous. Overused as a vague word of approval.

may. See *can.*

maybe, may be. *Maybe* is an adverb meaning "perhaps": *Maybe* you should ask her. Do not confuse it with the verb *may be*: He *may be* arriving late tonight.

media. See *data.*

meet up with. See *up.*

might of. See *could of.*

moral, morale. *Moral* (as an adjective) means "righteous, ethical": To pay his debts was a *moral* obligation.
Moral (as a noun) means "a lesson or truth taught in a story": The *moral* of the story is that greed is wrong.
Morale is a noun meaning "spirit": The team's *morale* sagged.

most, almost. Do not use the adjective *most* for the adverb *almost. Almost* (not *most*) all my friends came.

myself. See *herself.*

Harcourt Brace & Company.

nauseated, nauseous. *Nauseated* means "suffering from nausea": I was *nauseated* from the fumes.

Nauseous means "causing nausea": The *nauseous* fumes overcame me.

nice. Trite and overused as a substitute for *pleasant* or *agreeable* or for indicating approval. Use a specific adjective.

noplace, nowheres. See *anyplace*; *anywheres*.

notable, notorious. See *famous*.

nowhere near. Colloquial for *not nearly*.

number. See *amount*.

of. See *could of*; *kind of*; *kind of a*; *off of*; *outside of*.

off of. Usually redundant; omit *of*: Keep *off* (not *off of*) the grass. He jumped *off* (not *off of*) the platform.

O.K., okay. Colloquial for *all right* or *correct*.

one another. See *each other*.

only. Place *only* as close as possible to the word it modifies, to prevent misreading. "I *only lent* her those books" and "I lent her *only those* books" have different meanings.

or. See *and/or*.

oral. See *verbal*.

ought to of. See *could of*; *had ought*.

outside of. Colloquial for *besides, except*. *Of* is redundant when denoting space: She was *outside* (not *outside of*) the store. But "the *outside of* the house" is correct; here *outside* is a noun.

over with. Redundant; omit *with*.

party, person. See *individual*.

passed, past. *Passed* (verb) is from *pass*: I *passed* the test. *Past* (noun) means "a former time": Forget the *past*.

Past (preposition) means "by, beyond": Walk *past* the gate.

percent (per cent), percentage. Use *percent* (or *per cent*) with a specific figure: 45 *percent*. Otherwise, use *percentage*: a small *percentage* of voters.

personal, personnel. *Personal* means "private": It was a *personal* question.

Personnel are employees: Notify all *personnel*.

persuade. See *convince*.

phenomena. See *data*.

plan on. Do not use in formal English for *plan to*: I *plan to* go (not *plan on going*).

plenty. Colloquial when used as an adverb: His excuse was *quite* (not *plenty*) good enough for me.

Plenty is correct as a noun: We have *plenty* of food.

plus. In general writing, avoid using *plus* for *and*: Jill *and* (not *plus*) all her friends saw you. Jill saw you, *and* (not *plus*) she heard you sing.

practical, practicable. *Practical* means "useful, sensible, not theoretical"; *practicable* means "feasible, capable of being put into practice": Because they were *practical* women, they submitted a plan that was *practicable*.

precede, proceed. To *precede* is to come before: X *precedes* Y.

Proceed means "to go forward": The parade *proceeded*.

presence, presents. *Presence* means "being present; attendance": Demand their *presence*.

Presents are gifts, such as birthday *presents*.

pretty. Colloquial for *large*: The accident will cost him a *large* (not *pretty*) sum.

principle, principal. A *principle* is a rule or a truth (remember: *principLE* = *ruLE*): The Ten Commandments are moral *principles*. The Pythagorean theorem is a mathematical *principle*. Elsewhere, use *principal*, meaning "chief, chief part, chief person": All *principal* roads are closed. At 8 percent, your *principal* will earn $160 interest. The *principal* praised the students.

provided, providing. Use *provided* (*that*) in preference to *providing* when you mean "on the specific condition that": She will donate twenty dollars *provided that* (not *providing that*) her employer matches it.

quiet, quite. *Quiet* means "not noisy": This motor is *quiet. Quite* means "very, completely": I'm not *quite* ready.

raise, rise. *Raise, raised, raised* ("to lift, make come up") is a transitive verb (takes an object): He *raises* vegetables. He *raised* the window.

Rise, rose, risen ("to ascend") is an intransitive verb (never has an object): The sun is *rising.*

range, vary. *Range* means "to change or differ within limits": Applicants *ranged* in age from nineteen to thirty years.

Vary means "to change or differ": Applicants *varied* in age.

real. Colloquial when used for the adverb *really* or *very*: She was *very* (not *real*) brave.

reason is because. Redundant. Use *that* instead: The reason he is late is *that* (not *because*) he overslept. Or say *He is late because he overslept.*

regardless, regards. See *irregardless*; *in regards to.*

respectfully, respectively. *Respectfully* means "in a manner showing respect": He bowed *respectfully* before the queen. *Respectfully* yours.

Respectively means "each in the order given": First and second prizes were awarded to Luann and Juan, *respectively.*

Reverend. Never use *Reverend* alone as a form of address. The title *Reverend* is properly preceded by *the* and is followed by *Mr., Ms., Dr.,* or the first name or initials of the person referred to: We met *the Reverend* Charles Harris (or *the Reverend Mr. Harris*).

right. Colloquial or archaic when used to mean "directly" or "very": She went *directly* (not *right*) home. He was *very* (not *right*) tired.

right, rite, write. *Right* means "correct": the *right* answer.

A *rite* is a ceremony, such as an initiation *rite.*

To *write* is to put words on paper: *Write* us from Hawaii.

same. Unless writing a legal document, avoid using *same* for *it* or *them*: We visited Maine and found *it* (not *same*) delightful.

scarcely. See *can't hardly.*

seeing as how, seeing that. Incorrect for *since* or *because.*

seldom ever. Redundant and incorrect for *seldom, hardly ever, seldom if ever, seldom or never.*

shape. Colloquial if used for *condition*: He was in poor *condition* (not *shape*).

should of. See *could of.*

sight, site. See *cite.*

since. See *as, because, since.*

sit, set. *Sit, sat, sat* is an intransitive verb (has no object); it means "to be seated": I *sat* on the floor.

Set, set, set, is a transitive verb (has an object): it means "to put or place": She *set* the dishes on the table.

(*Set* has several intransitive senses, but it is equivalent to *sit* only when one speaks of a hen that *sets* on her eggs.)

so. *So* is informal when used to introduce a main clause; in formal writing, use *thus* or *therefore,* or recast the sentence:

Informal: All the crew died, *so* the ship was lost.

Formal: All the crew died; *thus* the ship was lost.

Recast: The ship was lost *because* all the crew died.

Avoid *so* for *very:* I am *very* (not *so*) happy.

Avoid using *so* for *so that* in clauses of purpose: She came *so that* (not *so*) she might help.

some. Colloquial if used for *somewhat, a little,* or *quite*: He worried *somewhat* (not *some*).

He's *quite* a (not *some*) golfer!

somebody, someone. See *anyone.*

Harcourt Brace & Company.

someplace, somewheres. See *anyplace*; *anywheres*.

sort of, sort of a. See *kind of*; *kind of a*; *these kind*.

stationary, stationery. *Stationary* means "not moving, not movable": This machine is *stationary*.

 Stationery is writing paper.

strata. See *data*.

such, no such a. *Such* is colloquial when used for *very*: It is *such* a lovely day. Better: It is a *very* lovely day.

 When *such* suggests "what kind" or "how much," it is followed in formal writing by a clause specifying the degree or kind: It was *such* a lovely day *that we went on a picnic.* We saw *such* clouds *that we came home.*

 No such a is incorrect for *no such.* There is *no such* (not *no such a*) place.

sure. Do not use the adjective *sure* for the adverb *surely* or *certainly*: I *surely* (not *sure*) admire her.

 Colloquial: "Are you going?" "*Sure.*"

sure and. See *try and*.

take. See *bring*.

take and, went and. Redundant: She *hit* (not *took and hit* or *went and hit*) the ball.

teach. See *learn*.

terribly. Colloquial when used for *extremely* or *very*: It's *very* (not *terribly*) late.

than, then. *Than* is a conjunction suggesting difference: He is taller *than* I (am tall). See also *different from*.

 Then is an adverb meaning "at that time," "next," or "in that case": *Then* we shall go.

that. See *being that*; *seeing that*; *this*; *this here*; *who*.

their, there, they're. *Their* is a possessive pronoun: It is *their* turn.

 There is an adverb referring to place: Sit *there*. It is also an expletive (an introductory word): *There* are four of us.

 They're is a contraction of *they are: They're* on their way.

them. Do not use for *those*: Watch *those* (not *them*) cars!

these kind, these sort. *Kind* and *sort* are singular nouns. Do not modify them with the plurals *these* and *those*. Use the singular *this* or *that* instead: I prefer *this* (not these) *kind* of fish. *That* (not *those*) sort of fish will make me sick.

thing. Avoid this vague noun where you can use a more specific one: Her next *point* (not *The next thing she said*) concerned economic benefits.

this, that, which. Use only to refer to a definite antecedent.

this here, that there, these here, those there. Nonstandard for *this, that, these, those.*

those kind, those sort. See *these kind*.

threw, through. *Threw* is the past of *throw*: I *threw* the ball. *Through* means "from end to end of." See also next entry.

through, thorough, thought. *Through* means "from end to end or side to side of": *through* the tunnel.

 Thorough means "complete, exact": a *thorough* search.

 Thought refers to thinking: a clever *thought*.

thusly. Incorrect for *thus*.

to, too, two. *To* is a preposition: She came *to* class. *To* also introduces an infinitive: I wanted *to* hear him.

 Too is an adverb meaning "also" or expressing degree: She laughed *too*. He was *too* sick to work. Do not use *too* for *very*: He did not look *very* (not *too*) happy.

 Two is a number: I have *two* books.

toward, towards. Use either, but be consistent.

try and, sure and. Incorrect for *try to* and *sure to*: *Try to* (not *try and*) come. Be *sure to* (not *sure and*) call me.

-type. Avoid needless or illogical use of *-type* as a suffix: She wanted a reflex (not *reflex-type*) camera.

Harcourt Brace & Company.

uninterested. See *disinterested.*

unique. *Unique* means "having no like or equal." Do not use it with *more, most, very,* or the like: The design was *unique* (not *most unique*).

up. Often redundant after a verb. Drop *up* unless dropping it changes your meaning: Connect (not *connect up*) the pipes. This road ends (not *ends up*) in a swamp. Climb (not *climb up*) that hill. Gerry and I met (not *met up with*) difficulties.

usage, utilize, use. *Usage* and *utilize* sound overblown if used where the simple *use* (noun or verb) will do. *Usage* means only "customary use or practice": The book explains English *usage. Utilize* means only "to put to some practical or special use": *Utilize* my cane as a splint. Otherwise, stay with *use.*

used to. The spelling is *used to,* except after *did:* They *used to* date. The flag *used to* have forty-eight stars. *Did*n't he *use to* smoke?

usually always. See *always.*

vary. See *range.*

verbal, oral, aural. *Verbal* means "expressed in words, either written or spoken": An artist's expression may take pictorial, plastic, *verbal,* or other form.
     Oral means "uttered or spoken": He gave an *oral* report.
     Aural refers to hearing ("of or perceived by the ear").

very. Do not use this adverb to modify a past participle directly. Use *very* + an adverb such as *much, well*: Her singing was *very much* appreciated (not *very* appreciated).
     Avoid overuse of *very. Extremely* and *quite* are good synonyms: She was *quite* (not *very*) embarrassed.

wait on. *Wait on* means "to attend or serve." It is colloquial if used to mean *wait for*: I waited *for* (not *on*) a bus.

way, ways. *Way* is colloquial if used for *far*: He lives *far* (not *way*) across the valley.
     Way is colloquial in reference to health: She is in *poor health* (not *in a bad way*).
     Ways is colloquial for *way* when indicating distance: She lives a little *way* (not *ways*) down the road.

weak, week. *Weak* means "not strong": *weak* from the flu. A *week* is seven days.

weather, whether. *Weather* refers to rain, sunshine, and the like.
     Whether introduces alternatives: *whether* we live or die.

weird. Slang when used for *strange, unusual.*

well. See *good.*

went and. See *take and.*

what. See *but what.*

where. Incorrect when used for *that.* I read in the paper *that* (not *where*) she had arrived.

where . . . at. See *at.*

whether. See *if; weather.*

which. See *this; who.*

while. The strict meaning of *while* is "during the time that." Avoid using it to mean *though* or *whereas*: A century ago many criminals were executed in America, *whereas* (not *while*) today very few are.

who, which, that. Use *who,* not *which,* when referring to people; *which* is only for things. *That* can refer to people or things: The people *who* (or *that,* but not *which*) live here are noisy.
     Who may introduce either a restrictive or nonrestrictive clause.
     That introduces only restrictive clauses. Many authorities say that *which* should introduce only nonrestrictive clauses, as in "Healy Hall, *which* is on your right, was built in 1878."

who's, whose. *Who's* is a contraction of *who is*: *Who's* that? *Whose* is the possessive of *who*: *Whose* hat is this?

with. See *over with.*

woman, women. *Woman,* like *man,* is singular: that *woman. Women,* like *men,* is plural: those *women.*

wonderful. Trite and overused as an adjective of approval.

Harcourt Brace & Company.

worst way. Incorrect for *very much*: I want *very much* to go (not *I want to go in the worst way*).

would have. Use *had,* not *would have,* in an *if* clause:
> Wrong: If I *would have* known, I would have left earlier.
> Right: If I *had* known, I would have left earlier.

would of. See *could of.*

write. See *right, rite, write.*

yet. See *but yet.*

you all. A southern regionalism for the plural *you.*

your, you're. *Your* is the possessive of *you*: Wear *your* hat. *You're* is a contraction of *you are*: *You're* late.

yourself. See *herself.*

you was. Nonstandard for *you were.*

Source: Blanche Ellsworth, *English Simplified,* 6th ed. (New York: HarperCollins, 1990), pp. 29–36.

Writing With a Word Processor

Most colleges and universities have writing labs equipped with computers, printers, and word-processing software. Today there is almost no excuse for not using these labor-saving tools, especially since a paper produced on a good computer is so much easier to revise and looks so much better in its final form. Even if you do not own your own computer, you should become familiar with a professional-quality word-processing program such as WordPerfect or Microsoft Word. You can learn such a program while working on a paper, and there are almost always people in the writing lab who will be willing to help if you get into a jam. It is a good idea to use the program to write short papers before tackling something more ambitious. Always make sure to back up your files on extra disks so that you do not lose precious research notes and written material as a result of damage or technical problems.

A computer-based word-processing system allows you to revise and polish your writing far more easily than was possible when each new version had to be retyped. Now you can afford to go back over the paper, especially those vital first paragraphs, until each sentence is as finely tuned as you wish. You can easily delete unnecessary words and replace tired clichés with more active words and phrases. You can quickly turn a sentence around so that the most important thought comes first. The computer can offer you no creative help in these matters, but it makes editing your work so easy that instructors are beginning to expect students to hand in more polished writing than they typically did in the past.

Most word-processing programs include spell checkers. But be warned: Spell checkers pick up only words that are misspelled. They do not check for agreement of subject and verb, or for words that are correctly spelled but out of place. If you use *their* when you mean *there,* the spell checker will not reveal the error. So use the spell checker, but remember that it is not a substitute for careful proofreading.

It is always a good idea to print out a rough draft and go over this "hard copy." You cannot see the whole essay or paper on a computer screen the way you can on paper. Also, you cannot as easily decide whether a portion of the paper needs more development or more cutting when you are looking at parts of the paper on a screen.

A final warning: Some students become overly involved in producing attractive papers using a variety of type fonts and other flourishes. This does no harm if you have already produced a first-rate, highly polished paper that meets the terms of the assignment and the standards of good writing. But instructors are highly skeptical of good-looking printouts that seek to mask superficial thinking and lazy editing. So use the word processor to help you be more efficient in your research and writing, not to cover up an inadequate job.

Harcourt Brace & Company.

References

Mills, C. W. (1959). *The Sociological Imagination.* New York: Oxford University Press.

Orwell, G. (1949). Politics and the English Language. In *The Orwell Reader.* Fort Worth, TX: Harcourt.

Parsons, T. (1951). *The Social System.* New York: Free Press.

Harcourt Brace & Company.

CHAPTER 1 Sociology: An Introduction

The Sociological Imagination
Sociology, the Human Science
    The Social Environment
    Levels of Social Reality
From Social Thought to Social Science
    The Age of Enlightenment
    The Age of Revolution
    The Great European Sociologists
    The Rise of Modern Sociology
Major Sociological Perspectives
    Interactionism
    Functionalism
    Conflict Theory
    The Multidimensional View of Society

Objectives

1. To understand the concept of the sociological imagination and the difference between personal troubles and social conditions.
2. To be able to apply the sociological imagination at different levels of complexity: micro, macro, and middle.
3. To be able to describe how the science of sociology developed during the nineteenth and twentieth centuries.
4. To become familiar with the basic sociological perspectives: interactionism, functionalism, and conflict theory.
5. To understand how modern sociological research combines the basic perspectives to create more powerful explanations of social conditions and social change.

Review

To test your comprehension of the material in the chapter, cover the words in the margin with a sheet of paper and fill in the blanks in the following summary. It is not always necessary to use exactly the same words as those in the margin.

Sociology is the __scientific__ study of human societies and of   [scientific]

human behavior in the __groups__ that make up a society. It is   [groups]

concerned with how __social conditions__ influence our lives as   [social conditions]

individuals. The ability to see the world from this point of view has been

Harcourt Brace & Company.

described as the _sociological imagination_   [sociological imagination]

Sociologists study social behavior at three levels of complexity.

Micro-level sociology deals with behaviors that occur at the level   [Micro-level]

of the individual and immediate others. The _middle_ level of   [middle]

sociological observation is concerned with how the social structures in

which people participate actually shape their lives. _Macro-level_   [Macro-level]

studies attempt to explain the social processes that influence populations,

social classes, and entire societies.

The scientific discoveries of the seventeenth century led to the rise of the

idea of _progress_, as opposed to the notion of human   [progress]

helplessness in the face of divine Providence. In the eighteenth century,

revolutions in Europe and North America completely changed the   [revolutions]

social order and gave rise to new perspectives on human social life.

Out of this period of social and intellectual ferment came the idea of creating

a _science_ of human society. Sociology developed in Europe   [science]

in the nineteenth century. During that formative period a number of

outstanding sociologists shaped and refined the new discipline. Among

them were _Karl Marx_, _& Émile Durkheim_, and   [Karl Marx, Émile

Max Weber.   Durkheim, Max Weber]

In the twentieth century sociology developed most rapidly in North

America, spurred by the need for _empirical_ information about   [empirical]

social conditions. Numerous _social surveys_ were conducted around   [social surveys]

the turn of the century. By the late 1920s two distinct approaches to the

study of society had evolved at American universities. The

Chicago School focused on the relationship between the individual   [Chicago school]

Harcourt Brace & Company.

and society, while the major East Coast universities leaned toward

_____ analysis. [macro-level]

Under the leadership of Robert Park and Ernest Burgess, the Chicago

school developed the approach known as _____. This [human ecology]

perspective emphasizes the relationships among social order, social

disorganization, and the distribution of populations in space and time. A key

concept in this perspective is _____. _____ is [community; Interactionism]

a perspective that views social order and social change as resulting from all

the repeated interactions among individuals and groups. One version of this

approach is _____ or _____ theory, which [rational-choice; exchange]

focuses on what people seem to be getting from their interactions and what

they contribute to them. Another version is the _____ [symbolic-interactionist]

perspective, which studies how social structures are actually created in the

course of human interaction.

_____ is concerned primarily with the large-scale structures [Functionalism]

of society; it asks how those structures enable society to carry out its basic

functions. In the decades since World War II this perspective has been

strongly challenged by _____, which emphasizes the role of [conflict theory]

conflict and power in explaining not only why societies change but also

why they hold together.

Matching Exercise

For each of the following terms, identify the correct definition and enter the appropriate letter in the blank in front of the definition.

a. sociology
b. social conditions
c. sociological imagination
d. micro-level sociology
e. macro-level sociology
f. middle-level sociology
g. scientific method
h. human ecology
i. interactionism
j. functionalism
k. conflict theory

___d___1. an approach to the study of society that focuses on patterns of social interaction at the individual level.

Harcourt Brace & Company.

_h_ 2.   a sociological perspective that emphasizes the relationships among social order, social disorganization, and the distribution of populations in time and space.

_K_ 3.   a sociological perspective that emphasizes the role of conflict and power in society.

_l_ 4.   an approach to the study of society that focuses on the major structures and institutions of society.

_j_ 5.   a sociological perspective that focuses on the ways in which a complex pattern of social structures and arrangements contributes to social order.

_f_ 6.   an approach to the study of society that focuses on relationships between social structures and the individual.

_b_ 7.   the realities of the life we create together as social beings.

_i_ 8.   a sociological perspective that views social order and social change as resulting from all the repeated interactions among individuals and groups.

_g_ 9.   the process by which theories and explanations are constructed through repeated observation and careful description.

_c_ 10.   according to C. Wright Mills, the ability to see how social conditions affect our lives.

_a_ 11.   the scientific study of human societies and human behavior in the groups that make up a society.

Self-Test

_d_ 1.   Which of the following is a characteristic of sociology?
a.   It is the study of human societies.
b.   It focuses on human behavior in groups.
c.   It uses scientific research methods.
d.   all of the above

_a_ 2.   A study of how people interact in telephone conversations would be an example of sociological research at the
a.   micro level.   c.   macro level.
b.   middle level.   d.   none of the above

_b_ 3.   Modern sociology originated in the scientific discoveries of the seventeenth century, which gave rise to a theory of
a.   divine Providence.   c.   natural selection.
b.   human progress.   d.   class conflict.

_b_ 4.   The term sociology was coined by
a.   Karl Marx.   c.   Émile Durkheim.
b.   Auguste Comte.   d.   Robert Park.

Harcourt Brace & Company.

_c_ 5. The early sociologists devoted much of their attention to
   a. conducting social surveys.
   b. studying patterns of behavior.
   c. developing macrosociological theories.
   d. analyzing census data.

_d_ 6. Karl Marx believed that the societies of his day would be transformed by
   a. natural selection.   c. technological innovations.
   b. changing cultural values.   d. violent revolutions.

_c_ 7. Which of the following early sociologists emphasizes the importance of bureaucratic forms of social organization in modern societies?
   a. Auguste Comte   c. Max Weber
   b. Robert Park   d. Karl Marx

_a_ 8. In the United States, the reform movements of the late nineteenth and early twentieth centuries gave rise to a demand for
   a. empirical research.   c. socialism.
   b. macro-level analysis.   d. sociology departments.

_d_ 9. The first black sociologist to gain worldwide recognition was
   a. Jacob Riis.   c. Ernest Burgess.
   b. Jane Addams.   d. W. E. B. DuBois.

_a_ 10. The distinctive orientation of the Chicago school was its emphasis on the relationships among social order, social disorganization, and the distribution of populations in space and time. This approach became known as
   a. human ecology.   c. functionalism.
   b. symbolic interactionism.   d. conflict theory.

_c_ 11. The sociological perspective that focuses on interpersonal behavior is
   a. functionalism.   c. interactionism.
   b. socialism.   d. none of the above

_b_ 12. The study of how people learn to play certain roles and how those roles are used in the social construction of groups and organizations is termed
   a. human ecology.   c. functionalism.
   b. symbolic ecology.   d. conflict theory.

_a_ 13. The functionalist perspective is concerned primarily with
   a. the large-scale structures of society.
   b. the role of conflict in social change.
   c. the micro level of interaction.
   d. the distribution of populations in space and time.

_d_ 14. The events of the world wars, the Depression, and the Holocaust gave impetus to the sociological perspective known as
   a. exchange theory.   c. functionalism
   b. symbolic interactionism.   d. conflict theory.

___d___ 15. Which of the following statements is correct?
    a. Each of the major sociological perspectives emphasizes different questions about social life.
    b. Much sociological research combines the insights of different perspectives.
    c. None of the major sociological perspectives can stand alone for very long.
    d. all of the above

T/F 16. The term "sociological imagination" refers to the ability to see how social conditions affect our lives and our times.

T/F 17. The revolutions of the eighteenth century produced drastic changes in the way people think and act as social beings.

T/F 18. The "social surveys" of the late eighteenth and early nineteenth centuries were an attempt to apply conflict theory to the study of industrialization and urbanization.

T/F 19. The Chicago school is closely associated with the development of the functionalist perspective in sociology.

T/F 20. Symbolic interactionism is the study of the process by which social life is constructed out of mundane acts of social communications.

21. Both sociology and psychology have to do with patterns of behavior. What is the key difference between the two disciplines?

_____

_____

_____

_____

22. In the 1950s Erving Goffman conducted a study of life in the Shetland Islands off the coast of Britain. He observed that in serving native dishes to a visitor from the mainland, a Shetland Island woman would listen politely to the visitor's claims of liking what he was eating, but at the same time would note the rapidity and eagerness with which he ate and use these signs as a check on what he said. What level of sociological analysis does this study represent?

_____

_____

_____

_____

23. In a controversial study entitled The Bohemian Grove, William Domhoff describes the lifestyle of the rich and powerful in the United States. He argues that the nation's top political and military leaders and corporate executives meet informally at exclusive clubs like the Bohemian Grove in California and make decisions that affect the lives of millions of people. Which of the major sociological perspectives is exemplified by this argument?

_____

_____

_____

_____

24. In Thomas Hobbes's famous fantasy, humans left to their own devices without the firm rule of a strong leader would descend into a "war of all against all." Show how the interactionist perspective, with both its rational-choice and its symbolic dimensions, would counter this gloomy prediction.

_____

_____

_____

_____

25. From the functionalist perspective, the disparity in earnings between the chief executive officer of a company and the hourly wage worker in the same company is necessary to provide the top manager with the incentives he or she needs to work hard and take necessary risks (as well as to compensate for past training and experience). Explain why this is a functionalist argument and how it might be criticized by a sociologist with a conflict perspective.

_____

_____

_____

_____

Harcourt Brace & Company.

CHAPTER 2   The Tools of Sociology

Applying the Sociological Imagination
Formulating Research Questions
Reviewing the Literature
The Basic Methods
Observation
Experiments
Survey Research
Research Ethics and the Rights of Respondents
Analyzing the Data
Frequency Distributions
Percent Analysis
Correlations
Mapping Social Data
Theories and Perspectives

Objectives

1. To be able to explain how sociologists go about studying society—that is, by constructing hypotheses and seeking answers through empirical study.
2. To appreciate the value of the basic sociological perspectives as guides in exploring existing knowledge about a research question.
3. To be able to describe various forms of sociological observation.
4. To be able to describe the use of experiments and their pitfalls.
5. To be able to explain the techniques used to conduct surveys and analyze data gathered in surveys.
6. To learn how to read and interpret tables.
7. To become aware of some of the ethical problems of social research.

Review

To test your comprehension of the material in the chapter, cover the words in the margin with a sheet of paper and fill in the blanks in the following summary. It is not always necessary to use exactly the same words as those in the margin.

The first step in designing social research is _____,   [formulating the

that is, asking a question about a social situation that can be answered   question]

through the _____ collection and analysis of   [systematic]

_____. Often the research question is expressed in the form   [data]

Harcourt Brace & Company.

of a _____, which states a relationship between two or more   [hypothesis]

variables that can be tested through empirical observation. The variable that

is to be explained is the _____. The other variable is the   [dependent variable]

_____.   [independent variable]

Before collecting new data, a professional researcher reviews as much

existing research and other data sources as possible. This

_____ sometimes supplies all the data necessary for a   [review of the literature]

particular study.

The most frequently used research methods in sociology are observation,

experiments, and surveys. Observation may take the form of

_____, in which the researcher participates to some degree in   [participant observation]

the life of the people being observed. It may also take the form of

_____, or observational techniques that measure behavior   [unobtrusive measures]

but intrude as little as possible into actual social settings.

_____ involves the use of photography and videotape to   [Visual sociology]

observe people in a variety of settings.

Sociological experiments can take one of two basic forms. In a

_____ the researcher establishes an _____,   [controlled experiment;

which will experience the "treatment" (a change in the   experimental group]

_____), and a _____, which will not   [independent variable;

experience the treatment. The effect of the treatment on the   control group]

_____ can be measured by comparing the two groups.   [dependent variable]

_____ take place outside the laboratory and are often used in   [Field experiments]

evaluating public programs designed to remedy specific social problems.

The "treatment group" consists of people who experience a particular social

program, and the control group consists of comparable people who do not

experience the program. A common problem of experimental studies is the

Harcourt Brace & Company.

_____, which refers to any unintended effect resulting from   [Hawthorne effect]

the attention given to subjects in an experiment.

The third basic method of sociological research, the survey, asks people to

give precise information about their _____ and   [behavior]

_____. The most ambitious surveys are   [attitudes]

_____; the data obtained by this means can be supplemented   [national censuses]

by smaller, less costly _____. A _____ is a   [sample surveys; sample]

selection of respondents drawn from a specific population. If each member

of the target population has an equal chance of being included in the sample,

it is a _____. The respondents in such a sample must be   [probability sample]

selected by some process of _____.   [random sampling]

_____ design is an important aspect of survey research.   [Questionnaire]

Questions must be precisely worded, easy to understand, and free of bias.

_____ require the respondent to select from a set of answers,   [Closed questions]

whereas _____ allow respondents to say whatever comes to   [open questions]

mind.

Sociological researchers must always consider the rights of human subjects.

_____ is the right to decide the terms on which one's acts   [Privacy]

may be revealed to the public. _____ means that the   [Confidentiality]

researcher cannot use the responses in such a way that they can be traced to

a particular respondent. _____ means that the respondents   [Informed consent]

must be told how the information they supply will be used and must be

allowed to judge the degree of personal risk involved in answering

questions.

The data gathered in a survey are usually presented in the form of statistical

tables. In reading a table it is important to know what the

_____ are and what kinds of data are being presented.   [units of analysis]

Harcourt Brace & Company.

_____ reveal the actual size of each category of a variable,   [Absolute numbers]

but to compare the numbers for different years it is necessary to calculate

_____. Data analysis often leads to the discovery of   [percentages]

_____, or specific relationships between two variables. Such   [correlations]

relationships should not be confused with _____.   [causation]

_____ of data about individuals or households provides a   [Mapping]

powerful new tool for analyzing sociological data.

Once data have been analyzed, they can be used to generate new

hypotheses. The types of hypotheses that might be developed depend on the

researcher's _____, a set of interrelated theories that offer   [theoretical perspective]

explanations for important aspects of social behavior. The functionalist,

interactionist, and conflict perspectives give rise to quite different

hypotheses. When new hypotheses have been suggested, the research

process begins anew.

Matching Exercise

For each of the following terms, identify the correct definition and enter the appropriate letter in the blank in front of the definition.

a. hypothesis
b. variable
c. dependent variable
d. independent variable
e. participant observation
f. unobtrusive measures
g. controlled experiment
h. experimental group
i. control group
j. field experiment
k. Hawthorne effect
l. sample

m. sample survey
n. closed question
o. open question
p. privacy
q. confidentiality
r. informed consent
s. frequency distribution
t. percent analysis
u. correlation
v. theory
w. theoretical perspective

___d___ 1.   a variable that the researcher believes causes a change in another variable.

___j___ 2.   an experimental situation in which the researcher observes and studies subjects in their natural settings.

Harcourt Brace & Company.

___n___ 3.   a question that requires the respondent to choose among a predetermined set of answers.

___l___ 4.   a set of respondents selected from a specific population.

___a___ 5.   a statement that specifies a relationship between two or more variables that can be tested through empirical observation.

___f___ 6.   observational techniques that measure behavior but intrude as little as possible into actual social settings.

___k___ 7.   the unintended effect that results from the attention given to subjects in an experimental situation.

___e___ 8.   a form of observation in which the researcher participates to some degree in the lives of the people being observed.

___i___ 9.   in an experiment, the subjects who do not experience a change in the independent variable.

___b___ 10.   a characteristic of an individual, group, or society that can vary from one case to another.

___o___ 11.   a question that does not require the respondent to choose from a predetermined set of answers. Instead, the respondent may answer in his or her own words.

___m___ 12.   a survey administered to a selection of respondents drawn from a specific population.

___q___ 13.   the promise that the information provided to a researcher by a respondent will not appear in any way that can be traced to that respondent.

___w___ 14.   a set of interrelated theories that offer explanations for important aspects of social behavior.

___c___ 15.   the variable that a hypothesis seeks to explain.

___s___ 16.   a classification of data that describes how many observations fall within each category of a variable.

___g___ 17.   an experimental situation in which the researcher manipulates an independent variable in order to observe and measure changes in a dependent variable.

___r___ 18.   the right of respondents to be informed of the purpose for which the information they supply will be used and to judge the degree of personal risk involved in answering questions, even when an assurance of confidentiality has been given.

___v___ 19.   a set of interrelated concepts that seeks to explain the causes of an observable phenomenon.

___h___ 20.   in an experiment, the subjects who are exposed to a change in the independent variable.

Harcourt Brace & Company.

_____t_____ 21.   a mathematical operation that transforms an absolute number into a proportion as a part of 100.

_____p_____ 22.   the right of a respondent to define when and on what terms his or her action may be revealed to the general public.

_____u_____ 23.   a specific relationship between two variables.

Self-Test

_____c_____ 1.   The first step in the sociological research process is
   a   reviewing the literature.
   b.   selecting a research method.
   c.   formulating research questions.
   d.   analyzing the data.

_____b_____ 2.   A relationship between two variables may be stated in the form of a
   a.   survey.   c.   perspective.
   b.   hypothesis.   d.   stereotype.

_____b_____ 3.   Before undertaking new research, the sociologist conducts a (an)
   a.   sample survey.   c.   controlled experiment.
   b.   review of the literature. d.   opinion poll.

_____d_____ 4.   A research method in which the sociologist becomes a member of the social group he or she is observing is
   a.   visual sociology.   c.   random sampling.
   b.   unobtrusive measurement.   d.   participant observation.

_____a_____ 5.   A research method that is often used to evaluate public programs that address specific social problems is the
   a.   field experiment.   c.   sample survey.
   b.   census.   d.   community study.

_____c_____ 6.   In a controlled experiment, the group that will experience a change in the independent variable is the
   a.   control group.   c.   experimental group.
   b.   sample group.   d.   random group.

_____d_____ 7.   In the Hawthorne experiments, the dependent variable was
   a.   lighting conditions.
   b.   coffee breaks.
   c.   communication between workers and managers.
   d.   worker productivity.

_____b_____ 8.   A full enumeration of every member of a society is a (an)
   a.   opinion poll.   c.   sample survey.
   b.   national census.   d.   market survey.

Harcourt Brace & Company.

_a_ 9. The first step in selecting a sample is to
  a. define the population to be sampled.
  b. establish rules for random selection of respondents.
  c. correct for sample bias.
  d. design the questionnaire.

_b_ 10. A percentage difference between two sets of responses that could be due to chance is known as
  a. sample bias.   c. random error.
  b. sampling error.   d. the Hawthorne effect.

_c_ 11. A question that requires the respondent to select from a set of answers is a (an)
  a. interview guide.   c. closed question.
  b. open question.   d. none of the above

_d_ 12. Changes in public opinion over time can be charted by means of a (an)
  a. national census.   c. percent analysis.
  b. cross-sectional survey.   d. longitudinal survey.

_a_ 13. Which of the following refers to statements made to respondents about what they are being asked and how the information they supply will be used?
  a. informed consent   c. confidentiality
  b. privacy   d. unobtrusive measurement

_c_ 14. Numbers that indicate how many observations fall within each category of a variable are
  a. percentages.   c. frequency distributions.
  b. random numbers.   d. correlations.

_d_ 15. Interactionism, functionalism, and conflict theory are the basic sociological
  a. theories.   c. hypotheses.
  b. correlations.   d. perspectives.

(T)/F 16. An empirical study is one that gathers evidence to describe certain kinds of behavior and to prove or disprove certain explanations of why that behavior occurs.

T/(F) 17. Participant observation is the most frequently used quantitative research method in sociology.

(T)/F 18. For both moral and practical reasons, sociologists do not have many opportunities to perform experiments.

(T)/F 19. The findings of a modern survey can be generalized from a small sample of respondents to an entire population.

T/(F) 20. The result of random selection of respondents is a biased sample.

21. What are the steps in the design and execution of a sociological research study?

_____

_____

_____

22.   The text refers to "reviewing the literature" as an important step in sociological research. What is the purpose and significance of this step?

_____

_____

_____

_____

23.   For each of the basic research methods described in the text, indicate the kinds of questions for which that method would be appropriate.

Participant observation:_____

_____

Unobtrusive measures:_____

_____

Controlled experiment:_____

_____

Field experiment:_____

_____

Survey research:_____

_____

24.   Suppose that you are going to design a brief questionnaire to determine what people feel about the problems of the earth's environment. How would you introduce the questionnaire to respondents to make sure you have given appropriate attention to the ethical aspects of research with human subjects?

_____

_____

_____

25.   Taking an example of your choice involving a variable that you wish to study, choose some other variables that you think help explain variations in the first variable. Describe these relationships in the form of statements about the dependent and independent variables, how you might measure them, and your main hypothesis or hypotheses.

_____

_____

_____

Harcourt Brace & Company.

CHAPTER 3 Culture

Objectives

1. To be able to define and apply the basic terms and concepts used in analyzing cultures.
2. To understand the relationship between culture and human evolution.
3. To be able to explain why language is central to the human ability to use culture in adapting to environmental conditions.
4. To appreciate the difference between cultures and civilizations and the tendency of civilizations to "export" their cultures to less powerful peoples.
5. To be able to use the concepts of acculturation, assimilation, and accommodation in explaining what happens when members of different cultures meet.

Review

To test your comprehension of the material in the chapter, cover the words in the margin with a sheet of paper and see if you can fill in the blanks in the following summary. It is not always necessary to use exactly the same words as those in the margin.

In the social sciences _____ refers to all the modes of   [culture]

thought, behavior, and production that are handed down from one

generation to the next by means of _____. Sociologists are   [communicative interaction]

Harcourt Brace & Company.

concerned primarily with aspects of culture that help explain

_____ organization and behavior.   [social]

Culture can be viewed as consisting of three major dimensions:

_____, _____, and _____   [ideas; norms; material

_____. _____ are the ways of thinking that   culture; Ideas]

organize human consciousness. Among the most important of these are

_____, socially shared ideas about what is right.   [values]

_____ are specific rules of behavior that are supported or   [Norms]

justified by values; _____ are norms that are included in a   [laws]

society's official written codes of behavior. _____ combine   [Ideologies]

ideas and norms; they are systems of values and norms that the members of

a society are expected to believe in and act upon without question. A

society's _____ consists of all the things it produces.   [material culture]

_____ combine norms and material culture; they are the   [Technologies]

things and the norms for using them that are found in a given culture.

_____ refers to the set of rules and understandings that   [Social control]

control the behavior of individuals and groups in a culture. The wide array

of norms that permit a society to achieve relatively peaceful social control is

called its _____. _____ are rewards and   [normative order; Sanctions]

punishments for adhering to or violating norms. Strongly sanctioned norms

are called _____, while more weakly sanctioned norms are   [mores]

known as _____.   [folkways]

One of the most hotly debated questions in the social sciences is how much,

if at all, human culture is determined by _____ factors.   [biological]

According to Darwin's theory of _____,   [natural selection]

_____ in organisms occur more or less randomly. Mutations   [mutations]

that enable an individual organism to survive and reproduce are passed on to the next generation. It is this process that permits animals and plants to

adapt to new _____.   [environments]

Herbert Spencer and other social thinkers, who came to be known as

_____, attempted to apply Darwin's theory to humans'   [social Darwinists]

ability to adapt to social environments. Spencer used the phrase

_____ to describe this ability. People who were able to   ["survival of the fittest"]

survive in the urban environment created by the _____ were   [industrial revolution]

viewed as superior human beings.

A more recent attempt to attribute social phenomena to biological processes

is _____. This term refers to efforts to link   [sociobiology]

_____ factors with the social behavior of animals. According   [genetic]

to the sociobiologists, such behaviors as incest avoidance, aggression, and

homosexuality may be genetically programmed in human beings. As yet

there is no evidence that such genes or sets of genes actually exist.

A more widely accepted view of culture denies that humans have

_____ and states that at a certain stage in prehistoric times   [instincts]

human culture became _____. Thus human evolution is not   [self-generating]

dependent on genes; instead, _____ techniques allow   [cultural]

humans to adapt to any physical or social environment.

The learning of culture is made possible by _____. Although   [language]

apes have been taught to use language to some extent, human language is

unique in that it allows its speakers to express an _____   [infinite]

number of thoughts and ideas that can persist even after their originators are

gone. According to the _____,   [linguistic-relativity

language also determines the possibilities for a culture's norms, beliefs, and hypothesis]

values. A less extreme form of that hypothesis recognizes the

_____ influences of culture and language.   [mutual]

Harcourt Brace & Company.

The notion that one's own culture is superior to any other is termed

_____. To understand other cultures it is necessary to   [ethnocentrism]

suspend judgment about those cultures, an approach termed

_____. Cross-cultural research has been used in efforts to   [cultural relativity]

find _____, traits that are found among humans everywhere.   [cultural universals]

Similarities among cultures have resulted from the processes by which

cultures spread across _____ and become part of a larger,   [national boundaries]

more advanced culture. A _____ may be defined as a cultural   [civilization]

complex formed by the identical major cultural features of a number of

particular societies.

A key feature of civilizations is that they invariably expand beyond their

original boundaries. The spread of civilizations can be explained by three

processes: _____, _____, and   [acculturation; assimilation]

_____. When people from one civilization incorporate norms   [accommodation]

and values from other cultures into their own, _____ is said   [acculturation]

to occur. The process by which culturally distinct groups within a larger

civilization adopt the language, values, and norms of the host civilization

and gain equal statuses in its institutions is termed _____. (If   [assimilation]

a distinct people fails to assimilate fully, it is referred to as a

_____; if it challenges the accepted norms and values of the   [subculture]

larger society, it may become a _____.) And when a smaller,   [counterculture]

less powerful society is able to preserve its culture even after prolonged

contact with a major civilization, _____ has taken place.   [accommodation]

Matching Exercise

For each of the following terms, identify the correct definition and enter the appropriate letter in the blank in front of the definition.

a. culture
b. ideas
c. norms
d. material culture
e. values
f. laws
g. ideologies
h. technologies
i. normative order
j. social control
k. sanctions
l. mores
m. folkways

n. natural selection
o. cultural evolution
p. social Darwinism
q. sociobiology
r. linguistic-relativity hypothesis
s. ethnocentrism
t. cultural relativity
u. civilization
v. acculturation
w. assimilation
x. subculture
y. counterculture
z. accommodation

___o___ 1. the process by which successful cultural adaptations are passed down from one generation to the next.

___s___ 2. the tendency to judge other cultures as inferior to one's own.

___b___ 3. the ways of thinking that organize human consciousness.

___q___ 4. the hypothesis that all human behavior is determined by genetic factors.

___l___ 5. strongly sanctioned norms.

___n___ 6. the relative success of organisms with specific genetic mutations in reproducing new generations with the new trait.

___x___ 7. a group of people who hold many of the values and norms of the larger culture but also hold certain beliefs, values, or norms that set them apart from that culture.

___h___ 8. the products and the norms for using them that are found in a given culture.

___r___ 9. the belief that language determines the possibilities for thought and action in any given culture.

___j___ 10. the set of rules and understandings that control the behavior of individuals and groups in a particular culture.

___a___ 11. all the modes of thought, behavior, and production that are handed down from one generation to the next by communicative interaction rather than by genetic transmission.

___g___ 12. systems of values and norms that the members of a society are expected to believe in and act on without question.

Harcourt Brace & Company.

_u_ 13.   a cultural complex formed by the identical major cultural features of a number of societies.

_c_ 14.   specific rules of behavior.

_y_ 15.   a subculture that challenges the accepted norms and values of the larger society and establishes an alternative lifestyle.

_p_ 16.   the notion that people who are more successful at adapting to the environment in which they find themselves are more likely to survive and to have children who will also be successful.

_z_ 17.   the process by which a smaller, less powerful society is able to preserve the major features of its culture even after prolonged contact with a larger, stronger culture.

_m_ 18.   weakly sanctioned norms.

_t_ 19.   the recognition that all cultures develop their own ways of dealing with the specific demands of their environment.

_i_ 20.   the array of norms that permit a society to achieve relatively peaceful social control.

_v_ 21.   the process by which the members of a civilization incorporate norms and values from other cultures into their own.

_d_ 22.   patterns of possessing and using the products of culture.

_w_ 23.   the process by which culturally distinct groups in a larger civilization adopt the norms, values, and language of the host civilization and are able to gain equal statuses in its groups and institutions.

_k_ 24.   rewards and punishments for abiding by or violating norms.

_l_ 25.   the ideas that support or justify norms.

_f_ 26.   norms that are written by specialists, collected in codes or manuals of behavior, and interpreted and applied by other specialists.

Self-Test

_d_ 1.   Which of the following is a cultural product?
   a.   Homer's *Iliad*   c.   the Declaration of Independence
   b.   a microwave oven   d.   all of the above

_a_ 2.   The ideas that support or justify norms are
   a.   values.   c.   technologies.
   b.   ideologies.   d.   institutions.

_d_ 3.   Laws forbidding murder and robbery are an example of
   a.   mores.   c.   formal norms.
   b.   folkways.   d.   both a and c

_C_ 4.   The originator of the theory of evolution was
   a.   Edward O. Wilson.   c.   Charles Darwin.
   b.   Herbert Spencer.   d.   William Graham Summer.

_b_ 5.   The view that it is impossible through intentional action to improve on the course of social evolution is known as
   a.   biological reductionism.   c.   creationism.
   b.   social Darwinism.   d.   ethnocentrism.

_b_ 6.   According to sociobiologists, the incest taboo is
   a.   a cultural norm.   c.   a folkway.
   b.   genetically programmed.   d.   determined by legislation.

_C_ 7.   The unique feature of human language is that
   a.   words can be used as symbols for things and relationships.
   b.   it can be learned through observation and imitation.
   c.   it can be used to express thoughts and ideas that can persist after their originators are gone.
   d.   None of the above is unique to human language.

_a_ 8.   The idea that language determines the possibility for thought and action in a culture is known as the
   a.   linguistic-relativity hypothesis.   c.   cross-cultural perspective.
   b.   sociobiological hypothesis.   d.   ethnolinguistic perspective.

_a_ 9.   The Europeans' belief that the native peoples of the "Indies" would benefit from contact with European civilization is an example of
   a.   ethnocentrism.   c.   assimilation.
   b.   cultural relativity.   d.   acculturation.

_C_ 10.   An advanced culture like that of ancient Rome is termed
   a.   a cultural complex.   c.   a civilization.
   b.   a subculture.   d.   an empire.

_b_ 11.   The process by which people incorporate norms and values from other cultures is termed
   a.   assimilation.   c.   accommodation.
   b.   acculturation.   d.   immigration.

_d_ 12.   Within the United States, people of Cuban origin may be described as a
   a.   civilization.   c.   microculture.
   b.   counterculture.   d.   subculture.

_b_ 13.   When a subculture that challenges the accepted norms and values of the larger society establishes an alternative lifestyle, it is called a
   a.   microculture.   c.   protest culture.
   b.   counterculture.   d.   social movement.

_d_ 14.   When one culture is wiped out by another, which of the following is said to have occurred?
   a.   acculturation   c.   accommodation
   b.   assimilation   d.   none of the above

___C___ 15.   When a smaller, less powerful society is able to preserve the major features of its culture even after prolonged contact with another society, which of the following is said to have occurred?
a.   acculturation   c.   accommodation
b.   assimilation   d.   resistance

T/F 16.   Social scientists are concerned primarily with such aspects of culture as literature and theater.

T/F 17.   Ideologies combine values and norms that all the members of a society are expected to believe in and act upon without questions.

T/F 18.   Laws, rules, and regulations are examples of informal norms.

T/F 19.   When applied to human societies, sociobiology has drawn severe criticism from both social scientists and biologists.

T/F 20.   Today the major focus of cross-cultural research is the search for "cultural universals."

21.   Define the various elements of culture and give an example of each.

_____

_____

_____

_____

22.   Explain what Herbert Spencer meant by "survival of the fittest." Give arguments for and against Spencer's belief that it is impossible to improve on the course of social evolution through intentional action.

_____

_____

_____

23.   The culture of a people shapes the consciousness of each member of the society in which that culture prevails. Explain this statement and give some examples to illustrate your explanation.

_____

_____

_____

24. Even though apartheid is no longer legal in South Africa, the idea that blacks and "coloreds" are inferior to whites remains ingrained in the culture of the white population. If you adhered to the concept of cultural relativity, how would you evaluate this feature of South African culture?

_____

_____

_____

_____

25. Three basic sociological concepts explain the spread of civilizations around the world. Define and give an example of each.

Acculturation:_____

_____

_____

Assimilation:_____

_____

_____

Accommodation:_____

_____

_____

CHAPTER 4   Societies and Nations

Objectives

1. To be able to define and explain the basic terms and concepts that sociologists use in studying social structure.
2. To understand how and why human societies have evolved from hunting-and-gathering bands to urban industrial nations.
3. To be able to distinguish between primary and secondary groups, role conflict and role strain, and ascribed and achieved status.
4. To understand how the concept of society differs from that of the nation-state.

Review

To test your comprehension of the material in the chapter, cover the words in the margin with a sheet of paper and fill in the blanks in the following summary. It is not always necessary to use exactly the same words as those in the margin.

A _____ is a population of people or other social   [society]
animals that is organized in a cooperative manner to carry out the major

functions of life. _____ refers to the recurring patterns   [Social structure]
of behavior that create relationships among individuals and groups within a

society. The "building blocks" of human societies are

_____—collections of people who interact on the   [groups]
basis of shared expectations regarding one another's behavior. In every

Harcourt Brace & Company.

group there are socially defined positions known as

_____. The way a society defines how an individual is   [statuses]

to behave in a particular status is called a _____.   [role]

An _____ is a more or less stable structure of statuses   [institution]

and roles devoted to meeting the basic needs of people in a society. Within

any given institution there are _____ that specify how   [norms]

people in various statuses are to perform their roles. New institutions

continually emerge through the process of _____.   [differentiation]

The growth of the world's population is directly related to the evolution of

human social structures, which in turn is related to changes in

_____. The first million years of human social   [production technologies]

evolution were characterized by a _____ way of life.   [hunting-and-gathering]

During that time the family and other kinship structures evolved, and the

_____ became the basic territorial unit of human   [band]

society. The shift to _____ is commonly linked with   [agriculture]

the invention of the plow, but for centuries human societies had been

acquiring food through the domestication of plants and animals. Some

became _____ societies based on the herding of   [pastoral]

animals, while others evolved into _____ societies   [horticultural]

based on the raising of seed crops. However, the first large-scale agrarian

societies evolved after the development of _____   [plow-and-harvest]

agriculture.

Agrarian societies allow people to escape from dependence on food sources

over which they have no control. In such societies, people produce

_____ that can be used to feed new classes of   [surpluses]

nonfood-producers such as warriors. At the same time, these societies

require increasing amounts of _____, and this may   [land]

lead to conflicts over territory. The need to store and defend food supplies

and to house nonfood-producers results in the growth of

_____ and _____.   [villages; small cities]

The next major change in human production technologies was the

_____, the shift from agriculture to   [industrial revolution]

_____ and _____. This began in   [trade; industry]

England around 1650 and spread to the United States and other nations in

the next two centuries. Its impetus came not only from technological

Harcourt Brace & Company.

advances but also from the rise of a new social order:

_____.   [capitalism]

The shift to industrial production affects social structure in several major

ways. As a result of the _____ of agriculture,   [industrialization]

relatively few people live on the land and increasing numbers live in cities

and suburbs. Greater openness to change results in the emergence of new

_____ and _____. Scientific and   [classes; social movements]

technical advances produce tremendous wealth, and the world "shrinks" as

a result of innovations in _____ and   [transportation]

_____.   [communication]

For the individual member of a human society, adaptation to a more modern

society entails a shift from _____ (close, personal   [gemeinschaft]

relationships) to _____ (well-organized but   [gesellschaft]

impersonal relationships). _____ like the family are   [Primary groups]

supplemented, if not replaced, by _____   [secondary groups]

(organizations or associations), whose members do not have strong feelings

for one another. Roles in secondary groups often conflict with roles in

primary groups, a situation known as _____.   [role conflict]

_____ occurs when a person experiences conflicting   [Role strain]

demands within a single role.

Another difference between simpler and more advanced societies is that in

the former almost all statuses are _____ (determined   [ascribed]

by birth or tradition), whereas in the latter there is a tendency to replace such

statuses with ones that are _____ (determined by a   [achieved]

person's own efforts). Sometimes a particular status takes precedence over

all of an individual's other statuses; such a status is referred to as a

_____.   [master status]

For most people in the world today, the word *society* suggests the

_____, or _____, of which they   [nation-state; nation]

are members. (A _____ is a society's set of political   [nation-state]

structures; a _____ is the territory within which those   [nation]

structures operate.) But although the members of a society often think of

themselves as members of a particular nation, this is not always so, and in

extreme cases the lack of a clear match between _____   [society]

and _____ can result in a civil war.   [nation]

Matching Exercise

For each of the following terms, identify the correct definition and enter the appropriate letter in the blank in front of the definition.

a. society
b. social structure
c. group
d. status
e. role
f. role expectation
g. institution
h. differentiation
i. pastoral society
j. horticultural society
k. social stratification
l. open society
m. closed society

n. capitalism
o. gemeinschaft
p. gesellschaft
q. primary group
r. secondary group
s. role conflict
t. role strain
u. ascribed status
v. achieved status
w. master status
x. state
y. nation-state

_____1.   a term used to refer to the close, personal relationships of small groups and communities.

_____2.   a society's expectations about how a role should be performed, together with the individual's perceptions of what is required in performing that role.

_____3.   the process whereby the members of a society are sorted into different statuses.

_____4.   a position or rank that is assigned to an individual at birth and cannot be changed.

_____5.   a collection of people who interact with one another on the basis of shared expectations regarding one another's behavior.

_____6.   a small group characterized by intimate, face-to-face associations.

_____7.   a society in which social mobility does not exist.

_____8.   conflict that occurs when the expectations associated with a single role are contradictory.

_____9.   a population that is organized in a cooperative manner to carry out the major functions of life.

Harcourt Brace & Company.

_____10.   a term used to refer to the well-organized but impersonal relationships among the members of modern societies.

_____11.   a social group whose members have a shared goal or purpose but are not bound together by strong emotional ties.

_____12.   a more or less stable structure of statuses and roles devoted to meeting the basic needs of people in a society.

_____13.   the recurring patterns of behavior that create relationships among individuals and groups within a society.

_____14.   the way a society defines how an individual is to behave in a particular status.

_____15.   the largest territory within which a society's political structures can operate without having to ace challenges to their sovereignty.

_____16.   a society in which social mobility is possible for everyone.

_____17.   conflict that occurs when in order to perform one role well a person must violate the expectations associated with another role.

_____18.   a society's set of political structures.

_____19.   a socially defined position in a group.

_____20.   a position or rank that is earned through the efforts of the individual.

_____21.   a status that takes precedence over all of an individual's other statuses.

_____22.   a society whose primary means of subsistence is raising crops, which it plants and cultivates.

_____23.   a system for organizing the production of goods and services that is based on markets, private property, and the business firm or company.

_____24.   a society whose primary means of subsistence is herding animals and moving with them over a wide expanse of grazing land.

_____25.   the process whereby sets of social activities performed by one social institution are divided among different institutions.

Self-Test

_____1.   Which of the following characteristics distinguishes a society from a population?
   a.   It is a set of individuals that can be counted.
   b.   It is organized in a cooperative manner.
   c.   It is made up of human beings.
   d.   all of the above

_____2.   The number of statuses in human societies is
a.   limited to approximately twenty.
b.   determined when the society is established.
c.   usually under 1000.
d.   infinite.

_____3.   People who hold the same statuses may behave in different ways, depending on how they perceive their society's
a.   social structure.   c.   role expectations.
b.   productive technologies.   d.   stratification system.

_____4.   An army platoon, a corporation, and the Girl Scouts are examples of
a.   organizations.   c.   statuses.
b.   groups.   d.   roles.

_____5.   For the first million years of human evolution, human populations sustained themselves by means of
a.   agriculture.   c.   hunting and gathering.
b.   domestication of animals.   d.   industrial production.

_____6.   A horticultural society is characterized by
a.   the raising of seed crops.
b.   the domestication of animals.
c.   plow-and-harvest agriculture.
d.   innovations in transportation and communication.

_____7.   A society in which a person is unable to move from one status to another is referred to as a (an)
a.   open society.   c.   gemeinschaft society.
b.   closed society.   d.   gesellschaft society.

_____8.   Which of the following is not associated with the industrial revolution?
a.   innovations in energy production
b.   the shift from agriculture to trade and industry
c.   the rise of capitalism
d.   a rapid increase in the number of women in the labor force

_____9.   The transition from an agrarian to an industrial social order is often described as a transition from
a.   an open society to a closed society.
b.   gemeinschaft relations to gesellschaft relations.
c.   secondary structure to primary structure.
d.   a horticultural society to a pastoral society.

_____10.   Town councils, school boards, and fund-raising committees are examples of
a.   primary groups.   c.   secondary groups.
b.   social classes.   d.   castes.

_____11.   A situation in which a student must break a date in order to study for an exam is an example of
a.   role conflict.   c.   role stress.
b.   role strain.   d.   none of the above

Harcourt Brace & Company.

_____12.   A situation in which an employee must miss a deadline in order to prepare a special
report is an example of
a.   role conflict.   c.   role stress.
b.   role strain.   d.   none of the above

_____13.   The status of black male is an example of an
a.   acquired status.   c.   achieved status.
b.   accidental status.   d.   ascribed status.

_____14.   The status of valedictorian is an example of an
a.   acquired status.   c.   achieved status.
b.   accidental status.   d.   ascribed status.

_____15.   A society's set of political structures is known as the
a.   state.   c.   nation-state.
b.   nation.   d.   government.

T/F   16.   The "building blocks" of societies are populations.

T/F   17.   Human societies rely on the creation of new statuses to adapt to social and
environmental changes.

T/F   18.   One of the key changes that occurred during the first million years of human
evolution was the establishment of social control of sexuality.

T/F   19.   Social stratification emerged as a result of the industrial revolution.

T/F   20.   Sociologists use the term *gesellschaft* to refer to the close, personal relationships
that characterize small groups and communities.

21.   Define group, status, role, organization, and institution, and indicate how they are related
to one another. Comment on the differences between the everyday meanings of these terms
and their sociological meanings.

_____

_____

_____

_____

22.   Draw the social structure of an organization of which you are a member. Draw what you
think might be the new structure if changes that might occur in the organization actually do
occur. Describe what these changes might be and why they are possible.

_____

_____

_____

_____

23.   Name some of the major advances that occurred during each stage of the evolution of human social structure.

Hunting and gathering:_____

_____

Agrarian:_____

_____

Industrial:_____

_____

24.   Modern society does not entirely eliminate gemeinschaft-type social organization. In fact, it is often the case that gemeinschaft relations arise in gesellschaft organizations. Explain this statement.

_____

_____

_____

_____

25.   Give three examples from the contemporary world in which members of a particular group within a nation-state think of themselves as forming a separate society.

_____

_____

_____

_____

Harcourt Brace & Company.

CHAPTER 5 Socialization

Objectives

1. To understand the meaning and implications of socialization as the process of "creating a social being."
2. To be able to describe various aspects of the nature-nurture issue.
3. To be able to discuss the stage theories of personality development proposed by Freud and Kohlberg, as well as interactionist theories of the formation of the self.
4. To appreciate the many contexts in which socialization occurs and the differing effects of various agencies of socialization.

Review

To test your comprehension of the material in the chapter, cover the words in the margin with a sheet of paper and fill in the blanks in the following summary. It is not always necessary to use exactly the same words as those in the margin.

_____ refers to the ways in which people learn to   [Socialization]
conform to their society's norms, values, and roles.

Harcourt Brace & Company.

_____ consists of the ways in which the newborn [Primary socialization]
individual is molded into a person who can interact with others according to
the expectations of society. _____ occurs in [Secondary socialization]
childhood and adolescence, primarily through schooling, and

_____ refers to the ways in which a person learns [adult socialization]
the norms associated with new statuses.

Among the most basic questions in the study of human socialization is that
of "nature" versus "nurture": To what extent does the development of the
person depend on genetic factors, and to what extent does it depend on
learning? The first social scientist to develop a theory that addressed this
issue was Sigmund Freud. Freud
believed that the personality develops out of the processes of socialization
through which the infant is gradually forced to control its

_____. He divided the personality into three [biological urges]
functional areas: the _____, from which [id]
unsocialized drives arise; the _____, which [superego]
incorporates the moral codes of elders; and the

_____, or one's conception of oneself in relation [ego]
to others.

In the growth of the personality, the formation of the
_____ or social self is critical. According to [ego]
Freud, this takes place in a series of stages in which conflict between the
demands of the _____ and those of the [superego]
_____ is always threatening to disrupt the [id]
functioning of the _____. [ego]

_____ asserts that all behavior is learned. It [Behaviorism]
originated in the work of _____, who showed [Ivan Pavlov]
that behavior that was thought to be instinctual could in fact be shaped or
_____ by learning situations. This line of [conditioned]
research was continued by _____, whose [John B. Watson]
experiments revealed the ability of conditioning to shape behavior in almost
any direction. Studies of _____, who have [feral children]
experienced extreme isolation or have been reared outside human society,
show that such children are able to learn but do so far more slowly than

Harcourt Brace & Company.

children who have not been _____ in early   [isolated]

childhood. Other studies have found that normal development requires not

only the presence of other humans but also the   [attention]

_____ and _____ of   [love]

adults. Children raised in orphanages and other nonfamily settings are more

likely to develop _____ problems and to be   [emotional]

retarded in their _____ development than   [language]

comparable children who are reared by their parents. Interactionist models

of socialization stress the development of the social self through   [interaction]

_____ with others. One of the earliest

interactionist theories was Charles Horton Cooley's concept of the   [looking glass self]

_____, the reflection of our self that we think we

see in the behaviors of other people toward us. This concept was carried   [George Herbert Mead]

further by _____, who emphasized the

importance of culture in the formation of the self. He believed that when

children play, they practice _____, or trying to   [role taking]

look at social situations from the standpoint of another person. This ability

develops through three stages. During the _____   [preparatory]

stage, children mimic the behavior of the _____   [significant others]

in their social environment. During the _____   [play]

stage, they play at being others who are significant in their lives. During the

third stage, the _____ stage, they develop the   [game]

ability to "take the role of the _____," that is, to   [generalized other]

shape their participation according to the roles of the other participants.

In playing the roles for which they have been socialized, people adhere to

the rules of interaction known as "_____." They   [face work]

seek to present a positive image of themselves, their

"_____," and to avoid being embarrassed, or   [face]

"_____."   [losing face]

_____ has proposed a three-stage sequence of   [Lawrence Kohlberg]

moral development in which the child's moral reasoning evolves from

emphasis on _____ and   [reward]

_____ to the ability to distinguish between   [punishment]

Harcourt Brace & Company.

_____ and _____.   [social laws; moral principles]
Studies of the environments in which socialization occurs have found that
normal development requires the involvement of one or more

_____ in the care of the child, as well as public   [adults]
policies that promote such involvement.

_____ are the groups of people, along with the   [Agencies of socialization]
interactions that occur within those groups, that influence a person's social
development. Within all agencies of socialization one finds a great deal of

_____, in which the individual plays at a role that   [anticipatory socialization]
he or she is likely to assume later in life.

After the _____, the most important agencies of   [family]
socialization are the _____. Other socializing   [schools]
agencies in the community include day care centers, churches, leagues, and
other associations. The dominant agency of socialization outside the family

is the _____, an interacting group of people of   [peer group]
about the same age. Such groups exert a significant influence on the
individual from adolescence on. The _____ are   [mass media]
another significant agency of socialization in American society.

The roles a person plays over a lifetime are influenced by

_____ change and by changes in the   [social]
_____ of their society. Socialization after childhood   [culture]
often occurs as a result of the influence of _____   [significant others]
and _____. A person's   [occupational mobility]
"_____" shapes that individual's responses to new   [core identity]
situations and challenges. _____ may occur at any   [Resocialization]
time during adulthood. Sometimes people undergo

_____ to correct patterns of social learning that   [resocialization]
they and others find detrimental. Erik Erikson focused on

_____, the social process whereby the individual   [identification]
chooses adults as _____ and attempts to imitate   [role models]
their behavior.

An important aspect of socialization is _____, or   [gender socialization]
the ways in which we learn our gender identity and develop according to

Harcourt Brace & Company.

cultural norms of _____ and   [masculinity]

_____. Gender identity is an individual's own   [femininity]

feeling of whether he or she is a _____ or a   [male]

_____.   [female]

Matching Exercise

For each of the following terms, identify the correct definition and enter the appropriate letter in the blank in front of the definition.

a. socialization
b. behaviorism
c. conditioning
d. feral child
e. id
f. superego
g. ego
h. role taking
i. significant other

j. generalized other
k. anticipatory socialization
l. agencies of socialization
m. agents of socialization
n. peer group
o. resocialization
p. total institution
q. identification
r. gender socialization

_____1.   a child reared outside human society.

_____2.   the ways in which we learn our gender identity and develop according to cultural norms of masculinity and femininity.

_____3.   according to Freud, the part of the human personality that is the individual's conception of himself or herself in relation to others.

_____4.   a theory that states that all behavior is learned and that this learning occurs through the process known as conditioning.

_____5.   a person's internalized conception of the expectations and attitudes held by society.

_____6.   the processes whereby we learn to behave according to the norms of our culture.

_____7.   according to Freud, the part of the human personality from which all innate drives arise.

_____8.   an interacting group of people of about the same age that has a significant influence on the norms and values of its members.

_____9.   individuals who socialize others.

_____10.   any person who is important to an individual.

_____11.   the social process whereby an individual chooses role models and attempts to imitate their behavior.

_____12.   the shaping of behavior through reward and punishment.

Harcourt Brace & Company.

_____13.   socialization that prepares an individual for a role that he or she is likely to assume later in life.

_____14.   according to Freud, the part of the human personality that internalizes the moral codes of adults.

_____15.   intense, deliberate socialization designed to change major beliefs and behaviors.

_____16.   trying to look at social situations from the standpoint of another person from whom one seeks a response.

_____17.   the groups of people, along with the interactions that occur within those groups, that influence a person's social development.

_____18.   a setting in which people undergoing resocialization are isolated from the larger society under the control of a specialized staff.

Self-Test

_____1.   Socialization that occurs when the child leaves the family for schooling and comes under the influence of adults and peers outside the household is known as
a.   primary socialization.   c.   adult socialization.
b.   secondary socialization.   d.   resocialization.

_____2.   The theory that asserts that all behavior is learned is known as
a.   sociobiology.   c.   behaviorism.
b.   biological determinism.   d.   identity theory.

_____3.   In Freud's model of the personality, the functional area that incorporates the moral codes of adults is termed the
a.   id.   c.   superego.
b.   ego.   d.   identity.

_____4.   Cases of feral children, or children who have been abandoned or isolated in infancy, show that
a.   isolation in childhood does not affect later socialization.
b.   socialization is unnecessary for a person to lead a normal life.
c.   socialization is a purely biological process.
d.   none of the above

_____5.   Comparisons of children raised in orphanages and other group settings with children raised in conventional families demonstrate the crucial role of which of the following aspects of socialization?
a.   initial intelligence   c.   nurturance and love
b.   early childhood education   d.   none of the above

_____6.   The concept of the "looking-glass self" was developed by
a.   Lawrence Kohlberg.   c.   George Herbert Mead.
b.   Jean Piaget.   d.   Charles Horton Cooley.

_____7.   A person who is an important figure in another person's social environment is referred to as a (an)
    a.   significant other.   c.   agent of socialization.
    b.   generalized other.   d.   peer.

_____8.   The individual's conception of the expectations of society and its demands is termed the
    a.   ego.   c.   significant other.
    b.   superego.   d.   generalized other.

_____9.   An example of face work would be
    a.   what a model does before appearing before the camera.
    b.   the universal language of facial gestures such as the "eyebrow flash."
    c.   the grim looks of basketball players who are losing an important game.
    d.   interaction in a small group designed to make a person feel better after spilling a dish in her lap.

_____10.   Perhaps the most influential researcher of moral development was
    a.   Ivan Pavlov.   c.   Erik Erikson.
    b.   B. F. Skinner.   d.   Lawrence Kohlberg.

_____11.   The groups of people that influence a person's social development throughout his or her lifetime are
    a.   a peer group.   c.   the generalized other.
    b.   agencies of socialization.   d.   resocializing agents.

_____12.   Situations in which an individual plays at a role that he or she is likely to assume later in life are known as
    a.   adult socialization.   c.   peer socialization.
    b.   anticipatory socialization.   d.   primary socialization.

_____13.   The primary agency of socialization is the
    a.   family.   c.   peer group.
    b.   school.   d.   mass media.

_____14.   The attitudes and values of adolescents tend to be most strongly influenced by their
    a.   teachers.   c.   peers.
    b.   siblings.   d.   parents.

_____15.   Erik Erikson's theory of personality development emphasizes the concept of
    a.   conditioning.   c.   delayed gratification.
    b.   identification.   d.   symbolic interaction.

T/F   16.   Today it is generally recognized that differences in temperament and personality are due entirely to biological factors.

T/F   17.   Sigmund Freud's theory of personality is based on the belief that the individual acquires a self by observing and assimilating the identities of others.

T/F   18.   Behaviorism traces its origins to the work of the Russian psychologist Ivan Pavlov.

T/F   19.   Lawrence Kohlberg's theory of moral development emphasizes the cognitive aspects of moral behavior.

T/F 20. People with greater genetic potential achieve more than people with less potential regardless of the environment in which they are reared.

21. Give some examples of socialization throughout the lifespan. What do these examples indicate about the idea that personality is determined by one's earliest experiences?

_____

_____

_____

_____

22. Sigmund Freud, Charles Horton Cooley, George Herbert Mead, and Erik Erikson all developed theories regarding the development of the personality. What is the central focus of each theory? Do you think they are mutually exclusive, or could the processes involved occur simultaneously?

_____

_____

_____

_____

23. Consider the peer group, the family, and the media, and show how the influences of each may reinforce or conflict with the influences of other agencies of socialization.

_____

_____

_____

_____

24. Think of a child you know. For that child, give an example of the agencies of socialization he or she now encounters. For each of those agencies, identify an agent of socialization (by status rather than by name).

_____

_____

_____

_____

25.   What is the significance of Claude Brown's description of the differences between his own view of his behavior (as a child) and his parents' view? How does this example highlight the effects of social change on basic socialization practices?

_____

_____

_____

_____

CHAPTER 6 · Interaction in Groups

The Importance of Groups
    Characteristics of Social Groups
    Group Size and Structure
    Communities
    Networks
Interaction in Groups
    Principles of Interaction
    The Economic Person Versus the Social Person
    Communication and Behavior in Groups
    Interaction and Group Structure
Formal Organizations and Bureaucracy
    Bureaucracy and Obedience to Authority
    Commitment to Bureaucratic Groups
Groups in Complex Societies
Research Frontiers: Why Americans Still Join Groups

Objectives

1. To be able to explain the concepts that organize sociological thinking about groups: primary and secondary groups, communities, in-groups and out-groups, and social networks.
2. To become aware of the major principles of group interaction.
3. To be able to apply the concepts of group structure and interaction to the study of formal organizations.
4. To understand the concept of bureaucracy.
5. To become aware that as societies change they become more "rationalized" and, hence, increasingly dominated by formal organizations.
6. To appreciate the fact that informal organizations can persist in bureaucracies and that communities can persist in highly bureaucratized industrial societies.

Review

To test your comprehension of the material in the chapter, cover the words in the margin with a sheet of paper and fill in the blanks in the following summary. It is not always necessary to use exactly the same words as those in the margin.

The social fabric of modern societies is composed of millions of

_____ of many types and sizes. Unlike a   [groups]

_____, a collection of individuals who are grouped   [social category]

together because they share a particular trait, a _____   [social group]

Harcourt Brace & Company.

is a set of two or more individuals who share a sense of common identity and belonging and who interact on a regular basis. Those interactions create a social structure composed of specific _____ and   [statuses]

_____.   [roles]

A _____ is characterized by intimate, often face-to-   [primary group]

face, association and cooperation. _____ are   [Secondary groups]

characterized by relationships that involve few aspects of the personality; the members' reasons for participation are usually limited to a small number of goals. As the number of people in a group increases, the number of possible relationships among the group's members _____ at a   [increases]

_____ rate. A group composed of only two people is   [faster]

known as a _____. The addition of a third person to   [dyad]

form a _____ reduces the stability of the group.   [triad]

At the level of social organization between the primary group and the institutions of the nation-state are _____.   [communities]

_____ are contained within geographic boundaries;   [Territorial communities]

_____ are networks of associations formed around   [nonterritorial communities]

shared goals. Territorial communities are usually composed of one or more

_____ in which people form attachments on the basis   [neighborhoods]

of proximity.

Groups formed at the neighborhood level are integrated into

_____ that may extend beyond geographic   [networks]

boundaries. A key factor in the formation of networks is

_____ _____ distinctions. Such   [in-group—out-group]

distinctions can form around almost any quality but are usually based on

such qualities as _____, _____,   [income; race]

or _____. Another type of group is the   [religion]

_____, a group the individual uses as a frame of   [reference group]

reference for self-evaluation and attitude formation. The study of who people associate with, how those choices are made, and the effects of those choices is known as _____.   [social network analysis]

Social scientists have identified certain principles of interaction that help explain both stability and change in human groups. Among them are the

_____ principle, the _____   [pleasure; rationality]

principle, the _____ principle, and the   [reciprocity]

_____ principle. The balance among these principles   [fairness]

Harcourt Brace & Company.

varies from one situation to another, with _____   [economic]

motives dominating in some instances and _____   [social]

needs winning out in others. From an interactionist perspective, an

important factor determining how people behave in a given instance is their

_____.   [definition of the situation]

Studies of interaction in groups use a variety of techniques.

_____ is the study of the underlying rules of behavior   [Ethnomethodology]

that guide group interaction. The _____ regards   [dramaturgical approach]

interaction as though it were taking place on a stage and unfolding in

scenes. The kind of strategies that people use to set a stage for their own

purposes is known as _____. Research on the   [impression management]

bystander effect has shown that when responsibility seems to be

_____, people are more likely to avoid helping others.   [diffused]

But when people define the situation as _____, they   [involving them]

will intervene despite the potential costs to themselves.

Research on small groups has shown that they tend to develop two kinds of

leaders, a "_____," who keeps the group focused on   [task leader]

its goals, and a "_____," who creates a positive   [socioemotional leader]

emotional climate within the group. _____ are groups   [Informal organizations]

with generally agreed-upon but unwritten norms and statuses, whereas

_____ have explicit, often written, sets of norms,   [formal organizations]

statuses, and roles that specify each member's relationships to the others

and the conditions under which those relationships hold. A

_____ is a formal organization whose members   [voluntary association]

pursue shared interests and arrive at decisions through some sort of

democratic process. A _____ is a formal organization   [bureaucracy]

characterized by positions with clearly defined responsibilities, the ordering

of positions in a hierarchy, governance by rules and precedents,

impersonality and impartiality, a career ladder, and efficiency as a basic

norm.

One effect of the increasing dominance of bureaucracies in modern societies

is the possibility that individuals will not take full

_____ for their actions. A study of obedience to   [responsibility]

authority conducted by _____ raised serious questions   [Stanley Milgram]

about people's ability to resist pressure to carry out orders for which they

are not personally responsible. Other studies have found that commitment

Harcourt Brace & Company.

by bureaucratic organizations is greatest when it is supported by

_____ or by strong _____   [ideology; primary-group]

attachments.

As a society becomes _____ and   [larger]

_____, it tends increasingly to be characterized by   [more complex]

secondary groups and organizations. These make the society more

_____, but they can also cause   [efficient]

_____ and _____. Durkheim   [confusion; unhappiness]

pointed out that members of complex societies have greater freedom to

choose _____ and   [what groups to join]

_____, but that they can be   [what norms to conform to]

overwhelmed by the choices open to them. Weber examined the effects of

the rise of bureaucracies in modern societies. He distinguished between

_____ motives, which are based on calculations of   [rational]

ends and means, and _____ motives, which are based   [traditional]

on the belief that certain actions are inherently right.

Matching Exercise

For each of the following terms, identify the correct definition and enter the appropriate letter in the blank in front of the definition.

a. social category
b. social group
c. primary group
d. secondary group
e. dyad
f. triad
g. community
h. territorial community
i. nonterritorial community
j. in-group

k. out-group
l. reference group
m. ethnomethodology
n. dramaturgical approach
o. impression management
p. informal organization
q. formal organization
r. voluntary association
s. bureaucracy

_____1.   the strategies one uses to "set a stage" for one's own purposes.

_____2.   a social group to which an individual has a feeling of allegiance; usually, but not always, a primary group.

_____3.   a network of relationships formed around shared goals.

_____4.   a set of two or more individuals who share a sense of common identity and belonging and who interact on a regular basis.

_____5.   a set of primary and secondary groups in which the individual carries out important life functions.

_____6.   a group that an individual uses as a frame of reference for self-evaluation and attitude formation.

_____7.   a group consisting of two people.

_____8.   a social group whose members have a shared goal or purpose but are not bound together by strong emotional ties.

_____9.   a social group characterized by intimate, face-to-face associations.

_____10.   any social group to which an individual does not have a feeling of allegiance; may be in competition or conflict with the in-group.

_____11.   a formal organization characterized by a clearly defined hierarchy with a commitment to rules, efficiency, and impersonality.

_____12.   a population that functions within a particular geographic area.

_____13.   a group consisting of three people.

_____14.   a group that has an explicit, often written, set of norms, statuses, and roles that specify each member's relationships to the others and the conditions under which those relationships hold.

_____15.   a formal organization whose members pursue shared interests and arrive at decisions through some sort of democratic process.

_____16.   a group whose norms and statuses are generally agreed upon but are not set down in writing.

_____17.   a collection of individuals who are grouped together because they share a trait that is deemed by the observer to be socially relevant.

_____18.   an approach to research on interaction in groups that is based on the recognition that much social interaction depends on the desire to impress those who may be watching.

_____19.   the study of the underlying rules of behavior that guide group interaction.

Self-Test

_____1.   Which of the following characteristics distinguishes true social groups from social categories?
   a.   They are collections of people who are in the same place at the same time.
   b.   Their members have a sense of belonging to the group.
   c.   Their members share a particular trait.
   d.   all of the above

_____2.   Which of the following are characterized by goal-oriented participation and relationships that involve few aspects of members' personalities?
a.   primary groups   c.   territorial groups
b.   secondary groups   d.   reference groups

_____3.   A group that consists of people whom one considers to be outside the bounds of intimacy is known as
a.   a primary group.   c.   a social network.
b.   a nonterritorial group.   d.   an out-group.

_____4.   A woman who finds a job in a bank and wears a tailored suit because she believes this is the proper attire for bankers is adhering to a standard set by her
a.   primary group.   c.   in-group.
b.   voluntary association.   d.   reference group.

_____5.   A study of interconnections among business leaders in major corporations would be an example of
a.   social network analysis.   c.   the dramaturgical approach.
b.   reference group analysis. d.   definition of the situation.

_____6.   People withdraw from participation in groups that they find unrewarding. This is an example of the
a.   rationality principle.   c.   pleasure principle.
b.   fairness principle.   d.   reciprocity principle.

_____7.   According to the rationality principle, people usually
a.   seek pleasure and avoid pain.
b.   expect that others will behave toward them the way they behave toward others.
c.   tend to make rough calculations of the costs and benefits of interactions with others.
d.   become angry when they do not receive certain kinds of treatment from others.

_____8.   The norms of the work group tend to be based on the
a.   fairness principle.   c.   rationality principle.
b.   reciprocity principle.   d.   pleasure principle.

_____9.   Experiments on the bystander effect have found that people are most likely to come to the aid of others when
a.   no one else is present.
b.   they define the situation as involving them.
c.   responsibility seems to be diffused.
d.   they are in no danger themselves.

_____10.   Studies of interaction in small groups have found that the person who initiates the most interactions often
a.   is the best-liked person in the group.
b.   gets no attention from the other members of the group.
c.   comes to be thought of as a leader.
d.   does not adhere to group norms.

_____11.   Positions with clearly defined responsibilities that are ordered in a hierarchy that constitutes a career ladder are characteristic of a
    a.   bureaucracy.   c.   reference group.
    b.   territorial community.   d.   voluntary association.

_____12.   In his experiments on obedience to authority, Stanley Milgram found that subjects were most likely to obey the experimenter when the "learner" was
    a.   in the same room as the subject.
    b.   in direct proximity to the subject.
    c.   in another room and could not be heard by the subject.
    d.   in another room but could be heard by the subject.

_____13.   A study of German soldiers captured during World War II found that the effectiveness of the German army was increased by the combat troops' tendency to form
    a.   strong ideological commitments.
    b.   close-knit primary groups.
    c.   an efficient organizational structure.
    d.   all of the above

_____14.   In simpler tribal or peasant societies all social structures are
    a.   primary groups.   c.   nonterritorial communities.
    b.   secondary groups.   d.   formal organizations.

_____15.   According to Max Weber, groups in modern societies are characterized by
    a.   primary motives.   c.   traditional motives.
    b.   secondary motives.   d.   rational motives.

T/F   16.   A primary group is distinguished from a secondary group by the fact that its members engage in face-to-face interaction.

T/F   17.   The size of the group is a significant factor in the maintenance of primary-group relations.

T/F   18.   In-group—out-group distinctions are usually based on meaningless qualities such as whether a teenager lives in a high-rise building or a garden apartment in the same neighborhood.

T/F   19.   Most of the time people's actions are based on fairness and what the group or society needs.

T/F   20.   Informal organizations have generally agreed-upon norms and statuses that are not set down in writing.

21.   The text defines several types of groups. Those types are listed here. In each case, briefly describe a group of which you are a member.

Primary group:_____

_____

Secondary group: _____

_____

Harcourt Brace & Company.

Territorial community: _____

_____

Nonterritorial community:_____

_____

In-group: _____

_____

Reference group:_____

_____

Informal organization:_____

_____

Formal organization:_____

_____

22.   Sociologists Vernon Boggs and Terry Williams have analyzed the con game known as three-card monte. They divide a typical monte episode into six predictable scenes in which an unsuspecting victim (such as a tourist on a crowded street) is induced to gamble and inevitably loses. Which approach to the study of group interaction does this analysis illustrate?

_____

_____

_____

_____

23.   Max Weber identified six key aspects of bureaucratic organizations. What are they?

_____

_____

_____

_____

24.   What are some reasons for the instability of the triad? Give some examples of unstable triads.

_____

_____

_____

Harcourt Brace & Company.

25.   If you had been a subject in the Milgram experiment, how do you think you would have behaved? Explain why you think you would have acted as you did, and compare your behavior to the categories of responses among Milgram's actual subjects.

_____

_____

_____

_____

CHAPTER 7   Deviance and Social Control

Objectives

1. To understand that deviance is a feature of all societies.
2. To be able to distinguish between deviance and stigma.
3. To appreciate the strengths and limitations of the functionalist approach to the explanation of deviance and criminality.
4. To be able to show how conflict and interactionist explanations of deviance and criminality differ from functionalist explanations.
5. To be able to discuss the measurement of crime by means of the Uniform Crime Reports and victimization surveys.

Review

To test your comprehension of the material in the chapter, cover the words in the margin with a sheet of paper and fill in the blanks in the following summary. It is not always necessary to use exactly the same words as those in the margin.

_____, broadly defined, is behavior that violates the   [Deviance]

norms of a particular society. The _____ label is   [deviant]

attached to a person who violates or opposes a society's most valued norms.

The ways in which a society prevents deviance and punishes deviants are

known as _____.   [social control]

There is usually much disagreement not only about which behaviors are _____ but also about which behaviors should be   [deviant]
_____ or   [condoned]
_____. An important dimension of   [punished only mildly]
deviance is the _____ of some groups in society to   [power]
define which acts are legal and which are illegal. Another dimension has to
do with _____ that a person cannot control, in contrast   [attributes]
to actual _____. In addition, some people are thought   [behavior]
of as deviant because of their membership in a _____   [group]
that deviates from the _____ of the larger society. To   [norms]
the rest of society they are deviants, but within the
_____ they are not.   [group]
Deviance should be distinguished from _____. A   [stigma]
_____ person has some attribute that is deeply   [stigmatized]
discrediting, such as a disfiguring disease. The study of deviance is
concerned with _____—that is, people who   [social deviants]
voluntarily violate the norms of their society. In particular, it focuses on
criminal deviance—acts or omissions of acts for which the state can apply
_____.   [sanctions]
As a culture's _____ and _____   [values; norms]
change, so do its notions of what kinds of behavior are deviant and how
they should be sanctioned. The extent to which the members of a society
agree on whether or not a particular behavior is deviant can range from
_____ (in cases in which there is much controversy)   [weak]
to _____ (in cases in which there is little   [strong]
disagreement). _____, or punishments, can range   [Negative sanctions]
from very weak to very strong.
A deviant _____ includes a system of values,   [subculture]
attitudes, behaviors, and lifestyles that are opposed to the
_____ culture of the society in which it is found.   [dominant]
Many _____ are harmful to society because they   [deviant subcultures]
sustain criminal occupations. Others provide opportunities to engage in
behavior that is pleasurable to many people but is considered deviant in
"_____" society. The boundaries between what is   [respectable]
normal and what is deviant are _____.   [not distinct]

Biological explanations of deviance relate criminality to

_____ or _____. These   [physical features; body

explanations influenced the earliest sociological explanations of deviance,   type]

which viewed crime and other forms of social deviance as varieties of

"_____" that could be attributed to the evils of city life.   [social pathology]

This view has been replaced by more objective and verifiable theories drawn

from the basic perspectives of modern sociology.

_____ theories of deviance include Robert Merton's   [Functionalist]

typology based on how people adapt to the demands of their society. In this

view, through socialization people learn what _____   [goals]

are approved of in their society and the approved _____   [means]

of achieving them. Individuals who do not accept either the

_____ and/or the _____ are likely   [approved goals;

to engage in deviant behaviors.   legitimate means]

Functionalist theories have been criticized for assuming that there is a single

set of _____ shared by all the members of a society.   [values]

Conflict theorists stress the relationship between _____   [cultural diversity]

and deviance. The two main types of conflict theories are cultural-conflict

theories and Marxian theories. Cultural-conflict theories concentrate on the

ways in which conflicting sets of _____ result in   [norms]

situations that encourage criminal activity. Marxian theories place more

emphasis on _____, explaining various types of crime   [class conflict]

in terms of the _____ position of those who commit   [social-class]

them.

Interactionist theories of deviance focus on the issues of

_____ (the question of why some people become   [recruitment]

deviant whereas others do not) and _____ (the creation   [production]

of new categories of deviance in a society). Edwin H. Sutherland's theory of

_____ holds that whether or not a person becomes   [differential association]

deviant is determined by the extent of his or her association with

_____. Interactionists believe that deviance is produced   [criminal subcultures]

by the process of _____, in which the society's   [labeling]

reaction to certain behaviors is to label the offender as a deviant. Once

acquired, such a label is likely to become incorporated into the person's

_____ and to increase the likelihood that he or she will   [self-image]

become committed to a "_____."   [deviant career]

Harcourt Brace & Company.

Studies of the incidence of crime often start from _____   [ecological]
data on crime rates. Studies of criminal _____, which   [victimization]
ask people about their actual experiences with crime, have made a major
contribution to the understanding of crime in complex societies.

The methods used to control crime change as societies become more
complex. In larger, more diverse societies the ability of local institutions to
control all of the society's members is _____. Such   [diminished]
societies tend to develop _____, more or less   [standardized]
_____, institutions to deal with deviants. Among the   [coercive]
most prominent institutions of social control in modern societies are courts
and prisons.

The primary functions of prisons are said to be _____,   [deterrence]
_____, and _____. However,   [rehabilitation; punishment]
prisons do not seem to deter crime, and only recently has the goal of
_____ been taken seriously. Numerous studies have   [rehabilitation]
found that prisons are not successful in rehabilitating their inmates and in fact
often serve as "_____." The only rehabilitation   [schools for crime]
programs that appear to be effective are those that give inmates
_____ and _____.   [job training; work experience]

Matching Exercise

For each of the following terms, identify the correct definition and enter the appropriate letter in the blank in front of the definition.

a. deviance
b. social control
c. stigma
d. crime
e. anomie
f. differential association
g. labeling
h. primary deviance
i. secondary deviance
j. recidivist
k. plea bargaining

_____1.   a theory that explains deviance as a societal reaction that brands or labels as deviant people who engage in certain behaviors.

Harcourt Brace & Company.

_____2.	the ways in which a society encourages conformity to its norms and prevents deviance.

_____3.	a process in which a person charged with a crime agrees to plead guilty to a lesser charge.

_____4.	an act or omission of an act that is prohibited by law.

_____5.	behavior that violates the norms of a particular society.

_____6.	behavior that is engaged in as a reaction to being labeled as deviant.

_____7.	a state of normlessness.

_____8.	an attribute or quality of an individual that is deeply discrediting.

_____9.	a criminal who is returned to prison after having served at least one term there.

_____10.	an act that results in the labeling of the offender as deviant.

_____11.	a theory that explains deviance as a learned behavior that is determined by the extent of a person's association with individuals who engage in such behavior.

Self-Test

_____1.	The ways in which a society prevents deviance and punishes deviants are known as
a.	stigmatization.	c.	social control.
b.	labeling.	d.	rehabilitation.

_____2.	Definitions of deviance are affected by
a.	differences in the power of various groups in society.
b.	whether a behavior is voluntary or involuntary.
c.	differences in values.
d.	all of the above

_____3.	Involuntary deviation from a norm of "respectable" society causes an individual to become
a.	stigmatized.
b.	a social deviant.
c.	a member of a deviant institution.
d.	none of the above

_____4.	Much of the study of social deviance focuses on
a.	crime.
b.	mental illness.
c.	eccentricity.
d.	membership in disvalued groups.

_____5.	Capital punishment is an example of a
a.	weak negative sanction.	c.	weak positive sanction.
b.	strong negative sanction.	d.	strong positive sanction.

_____6.   Biological explanations of deviant behavior are supported by evidence provided by studies of
a.   physical features such as prominent foreheads.
b.   variations in body type.
c.   genetic inheritance.
d.   none of the above

_____7.   Robert Merton sees the origins of deviance in
a.   individual pathology.   c.   poverty.
b.   effects of social structure.   d.   differential association.

_____8.   Marxian sociologists believe that deviant behavior occurs as a result of
a.   biological abnormalities.
b.   cultural differences.
c.   the exploitation of one social class by another.
d.   social dysfunctions.

_____9.   According to Edwin Sutherland, whether a person becomes a criminal or not is determined largely by the frequency of his or her contacts with people who engage in criminal behavior. This concept is termed
a.   labeling.
b.   secondary deviance.
c.   differential association.
d.   recidivism.

_____10.   Adherence to and dependence on the norms of a given social institution is termed
a.   recruitment.   c.   anomie.
b.   commitment.   d.   recidivism.

_____11.   Which of the following statements is not true?
a.   Crime rates are similar in all parts of the United States.
b.   The highest homicide rates are found in the southern states.
c.   Crime rates are related to the age composition of the population.
d.   Rates of homicide using firearms are similar in the United States and other Western nations.

_____12.   The probability that a person who commits a crime will be arrested, tried, and sent to prison is
a.   extremely likely.
b.   about 50 percent.
c.   about one in three.
d.   very low.

_____13.   The process in which a person who is charged with a crime agrees to plead guilty to a lesser charge and avoid a jury trial is known as
a.   revolving-door justice.   c.   plea bargaining.
b.   probation.   d.   deterrence.

_____14.   Studies of prisons have found that the function they fulfill most clearly is
a.   punishment.   c.   deterrence.
b.   rehabilitation.   d.   none of the above

_____15.   Critics of the prison system often focus on
      a.   the deterrent effects of prison.
      b.   the socialization that occurs in prisons.
      c.   the effectiveness of rehabilitation programs.
      d.   the need for capital punishment.

T/F   16.   A deviant person is someone who violates or opposes a society's most valued norms.

T/F   17.   Within a society there is usually considerable agreement about which behaviors are deviant and which are not.

T/F   18.   The population of social deviants is larger than that of stigmatized individuals.

T/F   19.   Victimization surveys show that the overall rate of serious crime is two to three times higher than the reported crime index.

T/F   20.   Current sociological explanations of social deviance are strongly influenced by the biological concept of disease.

21.   Give an example of each of the following: (a) a behavior that is considered deviant by one social group but acceptable by another; (b) a behavior that is considered deviant in one culture but normal in another; and (c) a behavior that was considered deviant in the past but is acceptable today.

a._____

b._____

c._____

22.   Compare and contrast the functionalist, conflict, and interactionist perspectives on deviance. How does each explain the existence of deviant behavior?

Functionalist:_____

_____

Conflict:_____

_____

Interactionist:_____

_____

23.   Define recruitment and commitment from the standpoint of deviant behavior. Can you apply these concepts to people with whom you are acquainted?

Recruitment:_____

_____

Harcourt Brace & Company.

Commitment:_____

_____

24.   In fighting crime there are usually limits to what formal law enforcement institutions can accomplish. What are some of those limits, why do they exist, and what can broader forms of social control contribute?

_____

_____

_____

_____

25.   Discuss the issue of labeling with regard to juvenile delinquents. Do you think that an early arrest can lead to further deviance? On what evidence do you base your conclusion?

_____

_____

_____

_____

CHAPTER 8   Collective Behavior, Social Movements, and Mass Publics

The Meanings of Disorder
The Nature of Collective Behavior
A Typology of Spontaneous Collective Behaviors
Dimensions of Social Movements
Social Movement Theory
A Continuum of Collective Behavior
Theories of Revolution
Protest Cycles, Action Frames, and Charisma
Social Movements and Civil Society
Resource Mobilization and Free Riders
Mass Publics and Public Opinion
Mass Publics
Public Opinion
Research Frontiers: Amusing the Millions

Objectives

1. To appreciate the fact that collective behavior and social movements are among the most important sources of social change in the modern world.
2. To be able to distinguish between spontaneous collective behavior and social movements.
3. To be able to define different types of social movements and discuss how such movements may develop and change over time.
4. To be able to discuss major theories of collective behavior and social movements.
5. To appreciate the importance of public opinion and mass publics in daily life.

Review

To test your comprehension of the material in the chapter, cover the words in the margin with a sheet of paper and fill in the blanks in the following summary. It is not always necessary to use exactly the same words as those in the margin.

The term _____ is used to refer to a continuum of   [collective behavior]

unusual or nonroutine behaviors that are engaged in by large numbers of

people. At one end of the continuum is the _____   [spontaneous]

behavior of people reacting to situations they perceive as uncertain,

Harcourt Brace & Company.

threatening, or extremely unattractive. At the other end are events that

involve large numbers of people in nonroutine behaviors but are

_____ by _____ and have   [organized; leaders]

_____. The set of organizations that plan such events   [specific goals]

is a _____   [social movement]

The study of spontaneous forms of collective behavior often begins by

distinguishing between a _____, a large number of   [crowd]

people who are gathered together in close proximity to one another, and a

_____, a large number of people who are all oriented   [mass]

toward a set of shared symbols or social objects. Collective behavior can

occur in crowds, in masses, or in both at once. The actual behavior that a

crowd or mass generates depends on the _____ people   [emotions]

involved feel are appropriate to express in those situations. The most

significant categories of emotions that motivate collective behavior are

_____, _____, and   [fear; hostility]

_____.   [joy]

Social movements have been classified into four types based on the goals

they seek to achieve. _____ movements aim to   [Revolutionary]

overthrow existing stratification systems and social institutions;

_____ movements seek partial changes in some   [reformist]

institutions and values; _____ movements attempt to   [conservative]

uphold the existing values and institutions of society; and

_____ movements seek to return to the institutions and   [reactionary]

values of the past. In addition, there are _____ social   [expressive]

movements, or movements devoted to the expression of personal beliefs

and feelings, and _____ movements, which are both   [millenarian] revolutionary and expressive. Within any large social movement there are

likely to be a number of different _____ or SMOs.   [social movement

Early theories of collective behavior were based on the notion that   organizations]

_____ or _____ feelings like   [hysteria; contagious]

hatred or fear could spread through masses of people. Gustav LeBon

attributed the strikes and riots common in rapidly urbanizing societies to a

_____ mentality created by the presence of large   [mob]

numbers of _____ in crowded cities.   [strangers]

Sociologists often distinguish between "_____," or   [long revolutions]

large-scale changes in the ecological relationships of humans to the earth

and to one another, and revolutions that are primarily social or political.

_____ are transformations in the political structures   [Political revolutions]

and leadership of a society that are not accompanied by a full-scale

rearrangement of the society's productive capacities, culture, and

stratification system. _____ not only change the   [Social revolutions]

institutions of government but also bring about basic changes in social

stratification.

According to Marx, revolutions would occur as a result of the spread of

_____: Impoverished workers and colonial peoples   [capitalism]

would rebel against the capitalists and create a _____   [classless]

society. In addition, Marx and de Tocqueville pointed to the role of

_____, noting that the feeling of deprivation relative to   [relative deprivation]

others—not the presence of deprivation itself—may give rise to

revolutionary social movements.

More recent analyses have shown that revolutionary social movements often

occur in _____ or _____. Waves   [cycles; waves]

of protest often result from major _____. During such   [social shocks]

Harcourt Brace & Company.

periods there is a dramatic increase in social conflicts, often motivated by

_____, or sets of beliefs and interpretations of events.   [collective action frames]

Successful leaders of social movements are often said to have almost

_____ powers to inspire and motivate their followers.   [supernatural]

Max Weber called this ability _____. Over time,   [charisma]

however, these leaders' goals must be incorporated into the structure of the

movement, a process that is referred to as the _____.   [institutionalization

However, the more successful the movement is, the more difficult it is to   of charisma]

maintain the zeal of its founders. In extreme cases the process can end in

_____, or efforts by an elite to control all forms of   [totalitarianism]

organizational life in a society.

The sphere of public, nongovernmental, nonbusiness social activity is

termed _____. People who participate in it are often   [civil society]

recruited into social movements. The _____   [resource mobilization

refers to the need to mobilize existing leaders and organizations rather than   question]

relying on the participation of people who happen to be moved to action. A

related issue is the _____ problem, the tendency of   [free-rider]

many people not to lend their support and resources to social movements

but to reap the benefits anyway.

In recent years activist groups have made increasing use of

_____ and the _____. Social   [laws; courts]

movements are more likely to use the tactics of _____   [protest]

when they are outside the framework of the law, but when laws have been

passed in response to their demands, they become more likely to initiate

_____ to achieve their goals.   [lawsuits]

_____ are large populations of potential spectators or   [Mass publics]

participants who engage in collective behavior of all kinds. Such factors as increased _____, the almost universal use of   [leisure time]

_____, and the technological revolution in   [automobiles]

_____ and the   [communications]

_____ have had an immense influence on the lifestyles   [mass media]

of mass publics, which in turn shape the society in which they live.

The presence of mass publics makes possible the emergence of

_____, or the values and attitudes of mass publics.   [public opinion]

The behavior that develops out of public opinion can take a variety of

forms, including _____, _____,   [fads; fashions]

and demands for particular _____. Public opinion is   [goods and services]

shaped in part by collective behavior, especially

_____. It is also affected by experiences shared by all   [social movements]

the members of society through the _____.   [mass media]

Matching Exercise

For each of the following terms, identify the correct definition and enter the appropriate letter in the blank in front of the definition.

a. collective behavior
b. social movement
c. crowd
d. mass
e. political revolution
f. social revolution

g. relative deprivation
h. charisma
I. civil society
j. modernization
k. mass public
l. public opinion

___h___1.   a special quality or "gift" that motivates people to follow a particular leader.

___l___2.   a set of changes in the political structures and leadership of a society.

___c___3.   a large number of people who are gathered together in close proximity.

___g___4.   deprivation as determined by comparison with others rather than by some objective measure.

___b___5.   organized collective behavior aimed at changing or reforming social institutions or the social order itself.

Harcourt Brace & Company.

_j_ 6. a term used to describe the changes that societies and individuals experience as a result of industrialization, urbanization, and the development of nation-states.

_d_ 7. a large number of people who are all oriented toward a set of shared symbols or social objects.

_c_ 8. the values and attitudes held by mass publics.

_f_ 9. a complete transformation of the social order, including the institutions of government and the system of stratification.

_k_ 10. a large population of potential spectators or participants who engage in all kinds of collective behavior.

_a_ 11. nonroutine behavior that is engaged in by large numbers of people responding to a common stimulus.

_i_ 12. the sphere of nongovernmental, nonbusiness social activity carried out by voluntary associations, congregations, and the like.

Self-Test

_a_ 1. Which of the following is *not* an example of spontaneous collective behavior?
a. a race riot   c. a run on a failing bank
b. a wildcat strike   d. a protest march

_d_ 2. Which of the following statements is true?
a. Social movements often grow out of more spontaneous episodes of collective behavior.
b. Collective behavior occurs in both crowds and masses.
c. The nature of an episode of collective behavior depends on the emotions that social situations bring forth.
d. all of the above

_c_ 3. A social movement that seeks partial changes in some institutions and values is a
a. revolutionary movement.   c. conservative movement.
b. reformist movement.   d. reactionary movement.

_d_ 4. A social movement that is devoted to the expression of personal beliefs and feelings is a
a. revolutionary movement.   c. reactionary movement.
b. reformist movement.   d. none of the above

_b_ 5. The People's Temple is an example of a
a. reformist movement.   c. reactionary movement.
b. millenarian movement.   d. revolution.

_a_ 6. Early theories of collective behavior were derived from the notion that industrial societies produce
a. a mob mentality.   c. relative deprivation.
b. charisma.   d. increased leisure.

__a__ 7.   The course of world history (as opposed to the history of individual nations) is shaped by
a.   long revolutions.   c.   political revolutions.
b.   social revolutions.   d.   none of the above

__c__ 8.   Modern theories of revolution are based on
a.   Weber's theory of institutionalization of charisma.
b.   Lofland's typology of collective behaviors.
c.   Marxian conflict theory.
d.   LeBon's analysis of crowd behavior.

__d__ 9.   When a social movement has incorporated the goals of its leaders into its structure, it is said to be
a.   reactionary.   c.   charismatic.
b.   institutionalized.   d.   totalitarian.

__b__ 10.   What proportion of American adults belong to voluntary associations?
a.   three-quarters   c.   half
b.   two-thirds   d.   one-third

__a__ 11.   The tendency of many people not to lend their support to social movements but to reap the benefits anyway is known as the
a.   free-rider problem.
b.   co-optation issue.
c.   institutionalization of charisma.
d.   tyranny of the majority.

__c__ 12.   Which of the following is not considered an indicator of modernity?
a.   urbanization
b.   the shift from agriculture to industry
c.   a longer work week
d.   increasing literacy

__b__ 13.   The formation of crowds, audiences, or streams of buyers and voters is characteristic of
a.   millenarian movements.   c.   long revolutions.
b.   mass publics.   d.   totalitarianism.

__c__ 14.   Which of the following is an effect of the development of mass publics?
a.   more time for leisure pursuits
b.   the technological revolution in communications
c.   the fast-food industry
d.   totalitarianism

__d__ 15.   An example of a behavior that develops out of public opinion is
a.   a fad.   c.   voting behavior.
b.   a fashion.   d.   all of the above

T/__F__ 16.   A mass is a large number of people who are gathered together in close proximity.

__T__/F 17.   Millenarian movements are both revolutionary and expressive.

T/__F__ 18.   A social revolution is a large-scale change in the ecological relationships of humans to the earth and to each other.

T/F   19.   The first modern theory of crowd behavior was developed by Gustav LeBon.

T F   20.   The theory of relative deprivation is used to explain the emergence of fads and fashions.

21.   Review Lofland's typology of spontaneous forms of collective behavior (Figure 8–1). Can you give examples of your own for each of the categories?

_____

_____

_____

_____

22.   Social movements have been classified into four categories based on their goal: revolutionary, reformist, conservative, and reactionary. Herbert Blumer has added a fifth category, expressive social movements. Give a current example of each type of movements.

Revolutionary:_____

_____

Reformist:_____

_____

Conservative:_____

_____

Reactionary:_____

_____

Expressive:_____

_____

23.   Distinguish among long revolutions, social revolutions, and political revolutions and give a current example of each. We hear frequent references to a "technological revolution." How would you classify this "revolution"?

_____

_____

_____

_____

24.   Why did many Eastern European countries have to rebuild their civil societies after the fall of the communist regimes in those countries?

_____

_____

_____

_____

25.   What are some steps that are taken in organizations and voluntary associations to address the free-rider problem? If you were organizing a social movement—say, to prevent overpopulation—what strategies would you employ to mobilize people?

_____

_____

_____

_____

Harcourt Brace & Company.

CHAPTER 9 Population, Urbanization, and Community

People, Cities, and Urban Growth
    The Population Explosion
    The Growth of Cities
The Urban Landscape
    Urban Expansion
    Metropolitan Areas
Urban Communities
    The Decline-of-Community Thesis
    The Persistence of Urban Communities
Cities and Social Change
    Inequality and Conflict
Research Frontiers: Coping With Disasters in Urban Communities

---

Objectives

1. To understand the equation for population change and the issues involved in the analysis of the worldwide population explosion.
2. To be able to describe the demographic transition as the central model for the demographic analysis of population growth and change in the modern world.
3. To understand the relationship between population growth and urbanization.
4. To be able to describe the Chicago school model of urban growth along with more recent theories of urbanization.
5. To understand the role of conflict in cities and its relationship to larger issues of social change.

Review

To test your comprehension of the material in the chapter, cover the words in the margin with a sheet of paper and fill in the blanks in the following summary. It is not always necessary to use exactly the same words as those in the margin.

Populations change as a consequence of _____,   [births]

_____, _____, and   [deaths; in-migration]

_____. The _____ is the   [out-migration; crude

number of births occurring during a year in a given population divided by   birthrate]

the midyear population. The _____ is the number of   [crude death rate]

deaths occurring during a year divided by the midyear population. The

Harcourt Brace & Company.

_____ is the difference between the crude birthrate and the [rate of reproductive change]

crude death rate for a given population. Since World War II the world

population has been increasing at an annual rate of more than

_____ percent, which means that by the year 2000 it will [1.5]

have passed _____. [6 billion]

The _____ is a set of major changes in birth and death rates [demographic transition]

that has occurred most completely in _____ nations in the [urban industrial]

past 200 years. It takes place in three stages: (1) _____ [high]

birth and death rates; (2) _____ death rates; and [declining]

(3) _____ birthrates. These stages are accompanied by [declining]

changes in the _____ of the population. [age composition]

Urbanization is closely linked with rapid increases in

_____, but at the same time the nature of life in cities [population]

tends to limit the size of urban _____. Cities grow [families]

primarily as a result of _____ (which is often caused by [migration]

population increases in rural areas), but new migrants do not find it easy to

form _____. [families]

The increasing tendency of people throughout the world to live in cities has

been referred to as the _____. Not only are increasing [urban revolution]

proportions of the world's population living in cities, but the cities

themselves are _____ than ever before. The growth of [larger]

cities in this century has given rise to the concept of the

_____, in which a central city is surrounded by a number [metropolitan area]

of smaller cities and suburbs that are closely related to it both

_____ and _____. [socially; economically]

The growth of cities should be distinguished from _____, [urbanization]

which refers to the proportion of the total population concentrated in urban

settlements. The result of urbanization is an "_____." Not [urban society]

only do cities serve as the _____ and [cultural]

_____ centers of such societies, but urban life has a [institutional]

pervasive influence on the entire society.

Sociologists have devoted a great deal of study to the processes by which

cities _____ and to patterns of _____ [expand; settlement]

within cities. An early model of urban expansion was the

_____ model developed by Park and Burgess. In this [concentric-zone]

Harcourt Brace & Company.

model a central business district is surrounded by successive

_____ devoted to light manufacturing, workers' homes,   [zones]

higher-class apartment buildings and single-family homes, and a

commuters' zone. This model is limited to _____ and   [commercial]

_____ cities that formed around business centers and does   [industrial]

not account for the rise of _____ cities and the rapid   [satellite]

urbanization that occurs along commercial _____   [transportation]

corridors. The growth of satellite cities was especially rapid before

_____. A more current model of urbanization is known as   [World War II]

_____ development and describes the incorporation of   [strip]

smaller communities and towns into a larger _____ area.   [metropolitan]

Metropolitan areas have expanded greatly since the mid-twentieth century,

largely as a result of the increasing use of _____ and the   [automobiles]

construction of a network of _____ covering the entire   [highways]

nation. In some areas this growth has created large multinuclear urban

systems that are described by the term _____. One effect   [megalopolis]

of the development of such areas is _____, in which   [decentralization]

outlying areas become more important at the expense of the central city.

Social scientists who have studied the effects of urban life have been

particularly concerned with the tension between _____   [community]

and _____ as it relates to life in cities. Early studies of   [individualism]

urban life tended to conclude that it weakens _____ and   [kinship ties]

produces _____ social relationships. Urban life was also   [impersonal]

thought to produce "_____" and _____.   [psychic overload; anomie]

More recently these conclusions have been criticized by researchers who

have found that many city dwellers maintain _____,   [stable]

_____ relationships with kin, neighbors, and coworkers   [intimate]

and that urban life is not necessarily _____ or   [stressful]

_____.   [anomic]

_____ sees the city as a mosaic of social worlds or   [Subcultural theory]

intimate social groups. Communities of all kinds can be found in cities.

Those communities may be based on _____,   [ethnicity]

_____, _____,   [kinship; occupation]

_____, or similar personal attributes.   [lifestyle]

_____ also have been found to be far less bored and   [Suburban dwellers]

isolated than was previously supposed.

Harcourt Brace & Company.

Occasionally various communities within cities come into conflict. Such

conflict may arise out of different _____ or the conflicting   [class interests]

goals of _____ within the city. Some urban sociologists   [groups]

see the city as divided into "_____" or territories whose   [defended neighborhoods]

residents attempt to protect them from "invasion" by outsiders.

Matching Exercise

For each of the following terms, identify the correct definition and enter the appropriate letter in the blank in front of the definition.

a. crude birthrate
b. crude death rate
c. rate of reproductive change
d. demographic transition
e. metropolitan area
f. urbanization
g. megalopolis

_C_ 1.   the difference between the crude birthrate and the crude death rate for a given population.

_f_ 2.   a process in which an increasing proportion of a total population becomes concentrated in urban settlements.

_d_ 3.   a set of major changes in birth and death rates that has occurred most completely in urban industrial nations in the past 200 years.

_g_ 4.   a complex of cities distributed along a major axis of traffic and communication, with a total population exceeding 25 million.

_a_ 5.   the number of births occurring during a year in a given population, divided by the midyear population.

_e_ 6.   a central city surrounded by a number of smaller cities and suburbs that are closely related to it both socially and economically.

_b_ 7.   the number of deaths occurring during a year in a given population, divided by the midyear population.

Self-Test

_b_ 1.   According to United Nations projections, by the year 2025 the earth's population may be

    a.   about the same as the current figure.   c.   about 2 trillion.
    b.   over 8 billion.   d.   drastically reduced.

_a_ 2.   The number of births occurring during a year in a given population divided by the midyear population is the
a.   crude birthrate.   c.   demographic transition.
b.   rate of reproductive change.   d.   basic demographic equation.

_c_ 3.   The first stage of the demographic transition consists of a (an)
a.   increase in death rates.   c.   decrease in death rates.
b.   increase in birthrates.   d.   decrease in birthrates.

_d_ 4.   Which of the following is not a factor in the demographic transition?
a.   higher age at marriage   c.   use of birth-control techniques
b.   fewer couples marrying   d.   urban–rural migration

_c_ 5.   The so-called urban revolution began
a.   in the sixteenth century.
b.   at about the same time as the shift to agriculture.
c.   around 1800.
d.   after World War II.

_d_ 6.   An urban society is characterized by
a.   expanding settlements.   c.   urban influence on rural areas.
b.   a mass culture.   d.   all of the above

_a_ 7.   The model of urban growth developed by Robert Park and Ernest Burgess was the
a.   concentric-zone model.   c.   strip development model.
b.   satellite model.   d.   none of the above

_b_ 8.   In which of the following does the town center eventually disappear?
a.   the concentric-zone model   c.   satellite cities
b.   strip development model   d.   the megalopolitan approach

_d_ 9.   The term megalopolis is used to describe an urban system characterized by
a.   multiple nuclei.
b.   a population over 25 million.
c.   a network of interdependent communities.
d.   all of the above

_c_ 10.   An important effect of the growth of megalopolitan areas is
a.   an increasingly homogenous population.
b.   more efficient public utilities.
c.   decentralization of business and industry.
d.   the demise of central cities.

_c_ 11.   Subcultural theory holds that
a.   urbanization leads to a decline of community.
b.   urban life creates "psychic overload."
c.   the city is a "mosaic of social worlds."
d.   rural life is much more pleasant than urban life.

_b_ 12.   Recent studies have found that suburban dwellers
a.   are bored and alienated.
b.   have little difficulty forming attachments.
c.   are ruled by strict conformity.
d.   none of the above

Harcourt Brace & Company.

_d_ 13.   Women who have lived in suburban communities all their lives
a.   find suburban life stifling.
b.   prefer to live in brand-new communities.
c.   feel that their opportunities are limited.
d.   none of the above

_a_ 14.   Which of the following statements is not true?
a.   Social change is less noticeable in cities than in rural areas.
b.   Urban renewal has given way to the concept of "redevelopment," which does not involve the destruction of entire neighborhoods.
c.   A "defended neighborhood" is a territory that a group of people are willing to defend against "invasion" by outsiders.
d.   A frequent source of intergroup conflict in American cities has been racial tension.

_a_ 15.   According to Kai Erikson, victims of natural and social disasters
a.   suffer sociological as well as economic and psychological loss.
b.   should be reimbursed only for property damage.
c.   have too much power relative to corporations.
d.   are powerless to confront corporations.

T/**F**   16.   Malthus attempted to show that population size normally increases more slowly than production of food and energy resources.

T/**F**   17.   The demographic transition is the difference between the crude birthrate and the crude death rate for a given population.

T/F   18.   Large-scale urbanization is a relatively recent development in human history.

T/**F**   19.   The concentric-zone model of urban expansion could not be applied to the growth of satellite cities.

T/F   20.   One effect of the growth of megalopolitan areas is decentralization, in which outlying areas become more important relative to the central city.

21.   What is the basic demographic equation? How do demographers use it to compare populations of different sizes?

_____

_____

_____

22.   Describe the three stages of the demographic transition and their effects on population size.

_____

_____

_____

Harcourt Brace & Company.

23.   Describe the classic Chicago school model of urban growth. Is it useful today? Why or why not?

_____

_____

_____

_____

24.   Compare the decline-of-community and subcultural theories of urban life. Which view is more valid, in your opinion?

_____

_____

_____

_____

25.   Why do societies often have a period of rapid population growth? What are some of the leading reasons that population growth might begin to level off?

_____

_____

_____

_____

CHAPTER 10   Global Social Change

Objectives

1. To appreciate the rapid pace of social change in the past half-century.
2. To be able to demonstrate how social change is experienced at the micro, middle, and macro levels of society.
3. To be able to discuss the impact of war and modernization in some detail.
4. To be able to relate theories of modernization and social change to the experience of change in the United States today.
5. To understand and apply the major theories of large-scale social change.

Review

To test your comprehension of the material in the chapter, cover the words in the margin with a sheet of paper and fill in the blanks in the following summary. It is not always necessary to use exactly the same words as those in the margin.

_____ refers to variations over time in the ecological   [Social change]

ordering of populations and communities, in patterns of roles and social

interactions, in the structure and functioning of institutions, and in the

cultures of societies. Such changes can result from forces building within

societies (_____) as well as from forces exerted   [endogenous forces]

Harcourt Brace & Company.

from the outside (_____). Changes at the   [exogenous forces]

_____, _____, and   [micro; middle]

_____ levels of social life usually are interrelated.   [macro]

No social change in human history has been as far-reaching and universal in

its consequences as the transition to an _____,   [urban]

_____ way of life. However, not all people who are   [industrial]

experiencing such changes think of them as _____.   [progress]

Nor can all forms of social change be _____,   [controlled]

although some changes are intentional. Similarly, while social scientists can

understand and predict the master trends of their era, they have limited

ability to anticipate major forms of change such as

_____, _____, or   [wars; social movements]

_____.   [technological changes]

One of the major forces that produce social change is

_____. The primary ecological effects of war are   [war]

_____ and _____. War also   [casualties; conquest]

results in large-scale shifts in _____ and rapid   [population]

acceleration of _____ change. It can affect a   [economic]

society's _____ in a variety of ways, and it may   [culture]

drastically change the structure of a society, especially its major social

_____.   [institutions]

_____ is a term used to describe a set of social   [Modernization]

changes that have taken place in societies throughout the world as a result of

industrialization, urbanization, and the development of nation-states. These

changes include a shift from simple techniques toward the application of

_____; an evolution from subsistence farming   [scientific knowledge]

toward the _____ production of agricultural goods; a   [commercial]

transition from the use of _____ and   [human]

_____ power toward the use of   [animal]

_____; and a movement from the farm and village   [power-driven machines]

toward _____. These processes may or may not take   [urban concentrations]

place simultaneously.

Some sociologists view _____ as a basic principle   [technology]

of social change. They recognize, however, that

_____ are often slow to adapt to changing   [social institutions]

technologies. This recognition forms the basis of the theory known as

_____. _____ critics argue [cultural lag; Post-

that technology and rationality deprive human lives of spirituality; they also modernist]

believe that major institutions of modern societies have become instruments

of _____ by _____. [social control; powerful

Social scientists often use the term _____ to refer to elites; Third World]

nations that have won independence from colonial dominance in the decades

since World War II. Such nations are also called

_____ or _____ nations. [developing; modernizing]

They are undergoing a set of transformations whose effect is to increase the

_____ of their people, their [productivity]

_____, their _____, and their [health; literacy]

ability to participate in _____. Wallerstein's world [political decision making]

system theory divides the world into _____ states, [core]

_____ areas, and _____ [semiperipheral; peripheral]

areas.

People often experience social change as highly _____. [problematic]

In pursuing new opportunities in education, leisure activities, intimate

relationships, and political participation, they may find themselves without a

clear set of _____ to guide their lives and hence may [norms]

experience _____. The entry of large numbers of [anomie]

women into the labor force, for example, has upset the traditional norms of

_____. Similarly, the civil rights movement has [family life]

greatly reduced racial discrimination in the United States, but for a large

proportion of the black population these gains have been offset by changes

in the _____. A third area in which social changes [structure of the economy]

touch the individual is _____, which may involve [public policy]

tradeoffs between conflicting goals such as eliminating poverty and

protecting the environment.

Sociologists have often attempted to develop models of social change that

can be used to predict the future of whole societies or civilizations. Many of

the founders of sociology favored an _____ model [evolutionary]

in which social change is seen as natural and constant; all societies

inevitably become increasingly _____ through a [complex]

steady series of stages. Modern evolutionary theorists refer to such models

as _____ because they predict that all societies will [unilinear]

Harcourt Brace & Company.

undergo the same process of change. _____ models   [Multilinear]

emphasize that one must study each society separately to discover the

evolutionary stages _____ to a particular society.   [unique]

A variety of theories have taken a _____ view of   [cyclical]

social change, in which civilizations rise and fall, respond to a series of

challenges, or alternate between two opposing sets of cultural values.

Conflict theorists argue that conflict among groups with different amounts

of _____ produces social change, which leads to a   [power]

new system of _____, which in turn leads to further   [social stratification]

_____ and further _____.   [conflict; change]

From a functionalist perspective, social change occurs as a result of

_____ growth, changes in   [population]

_____, social _____, and   [technology; inequality]

efforts by different groups to meet their needs in a world of

_____ resources. The latter two perspectives can be   [scarce]

applied to change at the _____ and   [micro]

_____ levels of social life as well as to   [middle]

_____ changes.   [macro-level]

Matching Exercise

For each of the following terms, identify the correct definition and enter the appropriate letter in the blank in front of the definition.

a. social change
b. endogenous force
c. exogenous force
d. modernization
e. cultural lag
f. developing nation
g. core state
h. semiperipheral area
i. peripheral area

_____1.   a term used to describe the changes that societies and individuals experience as a result of industrialization, urbanization, and the development of nation-states.

_____2.   pressure for social change exerted from outside a society.

_____3.   a region that supplies basic resources and labor power to more advanced states.

Harcourt Brace & Company.

_____4.   a nation that is undergoing a set of transformations whose effect is to increase the productivity of its people, their health, their literacy, and their ability to participate in political decision making.

_____5.   a technologically advanced nation that has a dominant position in the world economy.

_____6.   variations over time in the ecological ordering of populations and communities, in patterns of roles and social interactions, in the structure and functioning of institutions, and in the cultures of societies.

_____7.   a state or region in which industry and financial institutions are developed to some extent but that remains dependent on capital and technology provided by other states.

_____8.   pressure for social change that builds within a society.

_____9.   the time required for social institutions to adapt to a major technological change.

Self-Test

_____1.   Social change can result from forces exerted on a society from the outside. Such forces are referred to as
a.   peripheral.   c.   exogenous.
b.   cyclical.   d.   unilinear.

_____2.   Which of the following is an example of change occurring at the middle level of social life?
a.   changes in gender roles
b.   the rise of bureaucratic organizations
c.   urbanization
d.   all of the above

_____3.   Which of the following is not a characteristic of the modernization process?
a.   There is a change from subsistence farming toward the commercial production of agricultural goods.
b.   There is a transition from the use of human and animal power toward industrialization.
c.   There is a tendency toward the formation of urban concentrations.
d.   There is a trend toward a more humane and satisfactory way of life.

_____4.   The experiences of developing nations show that modernization is
a.   an inevitable process that occurs in all societies.
b.   essentially the same thing as secularization.
c.   likely to occur at different rates in different nations.
d.   usually limited to economic institutions.

_____5.   The general theory of development known as world system theory was proposed by
a.   André Gunder Frank.   c.   Miriam Wells.
b.   Immanuel Wallerstein.   d.   Arnold Toynbee.

Harcourt Brace & Company.

_____6.   In world system theory, an area that supplies basic resources and labor power to other nations is a
a.   peripheral area.   c.   core state.
b.   semiperipheral area.   d.   none of the above.

_____7.   Which of the following is not a challenge to theories of modernization?
a.   The rise of fundamentalism in the Middle East and elsewhere.
b.   The possible depletion of natural resources throughout the world.
c.   The steady increase in literacy rates in many regions of the world.
d.   The dependency of developing regions on core states for capital and technological expertise.

_____8.   According to Ralf Dahrendorf, a frequent effect of modernization on the lives of individuals is
a.   decreased political participation.
b.   a feeling of anomie.
c.   a higher level of living.
d.   unwillingness to face new experiences.

_____9.   Which of the following statements is true?
a.   About two thirds of all married women with children work outside the home.
b.   High-quality day care does not impede a child's development.
c.   The United States cannot be characterized as a "symmetrical society" in which men and women share equally in household and occupational pursuits.
d.   all of the above

_____10.   Which of the following is the primary explanation for the increasing gap between the haves and the have-nots in American society?
a.   changes in the economic structure of society
b.   legally sanctioned racial discrimination
c.   declining moral standards
d.   excessive population growth

_____11.   An assumption implicit in nineteenth-century models of social change is that
a.   people can create more perfect social systems.
b.   norms based on revered traditions should not change.
c.   all societies will eventually have institutions resembling those of Eastern Europe.
d.   Western Europe will always remain the dominant region of the world, and colonial powers will remain subordinate.

_____12.   Nineteenth-century models of social change tended to be
a.   cyclical.   c.   evolutionary.
b.   multilinear.   d.   homeostatic.

_____13.   Which of the following is not an example of a cyclical theory of social change?
a.   Spengler's "rise and fall of civilizations" thesis.
b.   Toynbee's "challenge and response" model.
c.   Sorokin's theory of alternation between ideational and sensate culture.
d.   Marx's theory of revolution brought about by class conflict.

_____14. Talcott Parsons's homeostatic model of society states that
   a.   conflict among groups and institutions is the primary source of social change.
   b.   a society's institutions function to maintain a state of equilibrium.
   c.   social evolution represents progress.
   d.   all of the above

_____15. Social change at the micro and middle levels of social analysis can best be explained by applying
   a.   the functionalist perspective.
   b.   conflict theory.
   c.   cyclical models.
   d.   all the basic sociological perspectives.

T/F   16.   Macro-level social change is most often experienced in communities, economic organizations, and governing bodies.

T/F   17.   Modernization refers to a set of social changes that societies and individuals experience as a result of industrialization, urbanization, and the rise of nation-states.

T/F   18.   Fundamentalist movements are found almost exclusively in the Islamic world.

T/F   19.   Changes in the environment are occurring more rapidly than changes in the political culture.

T/F   20.   Modern evolutionary theorists favor homeostatic models of social change.

21.   Summarize the social changes that are included in the concept of modernization. Do you think the developing nations will be able to complete the modernization process?

_____

_____

_____

_____

22.   Why does social change often lead to anomie?

_____

_____

_____

_____

23.   Name and describe some models of change that seek to predict the future of entire societies or civilizations. Do you think any of those models can fully explain the rise and fall of civilizations? Why or why not?

_____

_____

_____

_____

24.   Many people believe the old cliché that "history repeats itself." What support can be found for this idea in sociological models of social change? What evidence is there that this is an oversimplification?

_____

_____

_____

_____

25.   The United States has not been involved in a full-scale war since the early 1970s, yet it might be said that war continues to influence the course of social change. Expand on this idea with reference to current debates over military policy.

_____

_____

_____

_____

Harcourt Brace & Company.

CHAPTER 11 Stratification and Social Mobility

The Meaning of Stratification
Caste, Class, and Social Mobility
Life Chances
Stratification and the Means of Existence
Stratification in Rural Villages
Stratification in Industrial Societies
Stratification and Culture
The Role of Ideology
Stratification at the Micro Level
Power, Authority, and Stratification
Stratification in the Modern Era
The Great Transformation
Class Consciousness and Class Conflict
Social Mobility in Modern Societies: The Weberian View
Theories of Stratification
Conflict Theories
The Functionalist View
The Interactionist Perspective
Research Frontiers: Stratification and the World Economic System

---

Objectives

1. To understand the central concepts of social stratification: class, caste, ascribed and achieved status, open and closed societies, and social mobility.
2. To appreciate how closely social class is related to the ways in which people gain their living in different types of societies.
3. To understand the role of ideology in social stratification.
4. To be able to explain the concepts of power and authority, objective and subjective class, and class consciousness as they apply to stratification.
5. To be able to use examples of deference and demeanor to highlight the interactionist perspective on stratification.
6. To be able to apply the basic concepts of stratification to such social upheavals as the revolution against feudalism in France and the socialist revolution in the Soviet Union.
7. To recognize the importance of the concept of life chances and understand its relationship to stratification.

Harcourt Brace & Company.

Review

To test your comprehension of the material in the chapter, cover the words in the margin with a sheet of paper and fill in the blanks in the following summary. It is not always necessary to use exactly the same words as those in the margin.

_____ refers to a society's system for ranking people [Social stratification]

hierarchically according to various attributes such as

_____, _____, and [wealth; power]

_____. Societies in which there are rigid boundaries [prestige]

between social strata are said to be _____, whereas [closed]

those in which the boundaries are easily crossed are said to be

_____. Movement from one stratum to another is [open]

known as _____. [social mobility]

Most closed stratification systems are characterized by

_____, or social strata into which people are born and [castes]

they remain for life. Membership in a caste is an

_____ (a status acquired at birth), as opposed to an [ascribed status]

_____ (one based on the efforts of the individual). [achieved status]

Open societies are characterized by _____, which are [classes]

social strata based primarily on economic criteria. The classes of modern

societies are not _____; within any given class there [homogeneous]

are different groups defined by how much honor or prestige they receive

from the society in general. Such groups are sometimes referred to as

_____. The way people are grouped with respect to [status groups]

their access to scarce resources determines their

_____—that is, the opportunities they will have or be [life chances]

denied throughout life.

The principal forces leading to social stratification are created by the

_____ in a given society. Hence, for small farmers or [means of existence]

peasants (the majority of the world's population) social strata are based on

_____ and _____, with the [land ownership; agrarian

members of the lowest strata doing the hardest work while those at the top labor]

of the stratification system are able to live in relative comfort. Modern

industrials societies are characterized by _____ (the [structural mobility]

elimination of entire classes as a result of changes in the means of existence)

and _____ (the movement of individuals and groups   [spatial mobility]
from one location to another).

People accept their place in a stratification system because the system itself
is part of their society's _____. The facets of culture   [culture]
that justify the stratification system are learned through the process of
_____. The system is justified by an   [socialization]
_____. At the micro level, the norms of everyday   [ideology]
_____, especially _____ and   [interactions; deference]
_____, serve to reinforce the society's stratification   [demeanor]
system.

Changes in stratification systems may have as much to do with realignments
of social _____ as with economic or cultural changes.   [power]
_____ has been defined as "the probability that one   [Power]
actor within a social relationship will be in a position to carry out his or her
will despite resistance. Legitimate power is called
_____ and is a major factor in maintaining existing   [authority]
relationships among castes or classes.

The rise of _____ had far-reaching effects on   [industrial capitalism]
stratification systems. According to Karl Marx, capitalism divided societies
into classes based on _____.   [ownership of the means
The largest of these classes, the _____, must sell their   of production; workers]
labor to capitalists or landowners in return for wages. In time, Marx
predicted, the workers would become conscious of their
_____ and would rebel against the   [shared interests as a class]
_____. The outcome of the revolution would be a   [capitalist class]
_____. Marx defined social class in economic terms.   [classless society]
Max Weber took issue with this definition and pointed out that people are
stratified not only by wealth but also by how much honor or
_____ they receive from others and how much   [prestige]
_____ they command. Marx's view of stratification is   [power]
also challenged by studies of _____ in industrial   [social mobility]
societies, which have shown that there is considerable movement between
classes.

Modern conflict theorists, like Marx, believe that _____   [class conflict]
is a primary cause of social change. They disagree, however, on the nature

Harcourt Brace & Company.

of the _____ of capitalist societies. Functionalist   [class structure]

theorists believe that classes emerge because an unequal distribution of

rewards is necessary in order to channel _____ people   [talented]

into _____ roles in society. This view has been   [important]

criticized because it fails to account for the fact that social rewards in one

generation tend to improve the _____ of the next   [life chances]

generation; nor does it explain why talented people from

_____ families often are unable to obtain highly   [lower-class]

rewarded positions. From the interactionist perspective, the stratification

system is not a fixed system, but one that is created out of

_____.   [everyday behaviors]

Matching Exercise

For each of the following terms, identify the correct definition and enter the appropriate letter in the blank in front of the definition.

a. social stratification
b. closed stratification system
c. open stratification system
d. social mobility
e. upward mobility
f. downward mobility
g. caste
h. ascribed status
i. achieved status
j. class
k. status group
l. life chances

m. structural mobility
n. spatial mobility
o. status symbols
p. deference
q. demeanor
r. power
s. authority
t. objective class
u. subjective class
v. class consciousness
w. intragenerational mobility
x. intergenerational mobility

_____1.   a position or rank that is earned through the efforts of the individual.

_____2.   movement of an individual or group from one location or community to another.

_____3.   a social stratum into which people are born and in which they remain for life.

_____4.   a society's system for ranking people hierarchically according to such attributes as wealth, power, and prestige.

_____5.   the opportunities that an individual will have or will be denied throughout life as a result of his or her social-class position.

_____6.   a social stratum that is defined primarily by economic criteria such as occupation, income, and wealth.

Harcourt Brace & Company.

_____7.   a stratification system in which the boundaries between social strata are easily crossed.

_____8.   movement by an individual or group to a higher social stratum.

_____9.   material objects or behaviors that indicate social status or prestige.

_____10.   movement by an individual or group from one social stratum to another.

_____11.   power that is considered legitimate both by those who exercise it and by those who are affected by it.

_____12.   a change in the social class of family members from one generation to the next.

_____13.   the ways in which individuals present themselves to others through body language, dress, speech, and manners.

_____14.   movement of an individual or group from one social stratum to another that is caused by the elimination of an entire class as a result of changes in the means of existence.

_____15.   a stratification system in which there are rigid boundaries between social strata.

_____16.   in Marxian theory, the way members of a given social class perceive their situation as a class.

_____17.   a position or rank that is assigned to an individual at birth and cannot be changed.

_____18.   a group's shared subjective awareness of its objective situation as a class.

_____19.   a change in the social class of an individual within his or her own lifetime.

_____20.   the respect and esteem shown to an individual.

_____21.   the ability to control the behavior of others, even against their will.

_____22.   movement by an individual or group to a lower social stratum.

_____23.   in Marxian theory, a social class that has a visible, specific relationship to the means of production.

_____24.   a category of people within a social class, defined by how much honor or prestige they receive from the society in general.

Self-Test

_____1.   Numerous social scientific studies have demonstrated that some form of inequality can be found in
a.   hunting-and-gathering societies.   c.   industrial societies.
b.   agrarian societies.   d.   all human societies.

Harcourt Brace & Company.

_____2.   A society in which there are rigid boundaries between the various social strata is said to have
    a.   a closed stratification system.   c.   upward mobility.
    b.   an open stratification system.   d.   downward mobility.

_____3.   Social strata that are based primarily on economic criteria are known as
    a.   castes.   c.   status groups.
    b.   classes.   d.   all of the above

_____4.   The most basic set of forces that produce stratification is
    a.   ideological teachings.
    b.   the way people earn their living.
    c.   deference and demeanor.
    d.   conflicts among groups with different degrees of power.

_____5.   The industrial revolution brought about a tremendous increase in
    a.   structural mobility.   c.   both a and b
    b.   spatial mobility.   d.   neither a nor b

_____6.   Ideologies socialize new generations to believe that existing patterns of equality are
    a.   discriminatory.   c.   obsolete.
    b.   legitimate.   d.   irrelevant.

_____7.   The use of terms of address such as "Your Highness" or "Sir" is a way of showing
    a.   deference.   c.   class consciousness.
    b.   authority.   d.   social mobility.

_____8.   Power that is recognized as legitimate is known as
    a.   deference.   c.   ascribed status.
    b.   authority.   d.   achieved status.

_____9.   Which of the following became a dominant institution as a result of the industrial revolution?
    a.   the family   c.   democracy
    b.   religion   d.   markets

_____10.   According to Karl Marx, a class that has a visible, specific relationship to the means of production is
    a.   a caste.   c.   an objective class.
    b.   an open stratification system.   d.   a subjective class.

_____11.   According to Max Weber, people are stratified not only by their wealth but also by their
    a.   power and prestige.   c.   gender and age.
    b.   income and occupation.   d.   race and ethnicity.

_____12.   The chances of rising or falling from one social class to another within one's own lifetime are referred to as
    a.   intragenerational mobility.   c.   structural mobility.
    b.   intergenerational mobility.   d.   spatial mobility.

_____13.   Modern conflict theorists
    a.   agree that class conflict is a primary cause of social change.
    b.   disagree on the nature of the class structure.
    c.   disagree on the forms that class conflict takes.
    d.   all of the above

_____14.   The theory that social classes emerge because an unequal distribution of rewards is essential in complex societies is characteristic of
    a.   conflict theory.   c.   the interactionist perspective.
    b.   the functionalist perspective.   d.   Marxian socialism.

_____15.   The perspective that is most useful in explaining the prestige stratification that occurs within social classes is
    a.   conflict theory.   c.   the interactionist perspective.
    b.   the functionalist perspective.   d.   none of the above

T/F   16.   Soviet sociologists found little evidence of social inequality under communism.

T/F   17.   Castes are social strata into which people are born and in which they remain for life.

T/F   18.   The mechanization of agriculture increased the number of people needed to work on the land, thereby creating a new class of farm laborers.

T/F   19.   Demeanor refers to such clues as body language, dress, speech, and manners, which indicate how much respect we believe we deserve.

T/F   20.   The rise of capitalism largely destroyed the stratification systems of feudal societies.

21.   The chapter opens with a discussion of the social changes occurring in Russia. What implications do those changes have for stratification in Russian society?

_____

_____

_____

_____

22.   Distinguish between open and closed stratification systems and between castes and classes. Give an example of each.

_____

_____

_____

_____

23.   In addition to the increasing dominance of markets, the text lists five key elements of the Great Transformation. What are those elements?

(1)_____

(2)_____

(3)_____

(4)_____

(5)_____

How did these changes affect stratification systems in industrializing countries?

_____

_____

_____

_____

24.   What are some of the differences between castes, estates, and classes?

_____

_____

_____

_____

25.   Max Weber once said, in speaking about power and authority, "You can't sit on bayonets." Use the concept of legitimate authority to explain that statement.

_____

_____

_____

_____

CHAPTER 12 Inequalities of Social Class

Objectives

1. To review the concepts of caste and class, social mobility, and power and prestige.
2. To appreciate the importance of wealth, income, occupational prestige, and educational attainment as measures of inequality.
3. To become aware of how patterns of social-class stratification in the United States have changed as the nation has been transformed from an agricultural to an urban industrial society.
4. To be able to distinguish between subjective and objective measures of class membership.
5. To be able to describe the variations in life chances and lifestyles among the major social classes in the United States.
6. To become aware of the effect of women's participation in the labor force on the social mobility of families.

Review

To test your comprehension of the material in the chapter, cover the words in the margin with a sheet of paper and fill in the blanks in the following summary. It is not always necessary to use exactly the same words as those in the margin.

The basic measures of inequality in any society are

_____, _____,   [income; wealth]

_____, and   [occupational prestige]

Harcourt Brace & Company.

_____. In American society the distribution   [educational attainment]

of _____ and   [educational attainment]

_____ is more nearly equal than   [occupational prestige]

the distribution of _____ and   [wealth]

_____.   [income]

Sociological views of inequality in America have changed as the nation has

been transformed from an agrarian society to an urban industrial society and

then to a postindustrial society. The _____ view of   [Jeffersonian]

America envisioned a society in which most families lived on their own

farms or ran small commercial or manufacturing enterprises. However, this

view did not apply to the _____, the   [larger cities]

_____, or _____.   [southern states; Native

During the Great Depression, the effects of _____   Americans; industrial-

tended to increase hostility between the major economic classes in American   ization]

society, particularly between _____ and the   [workers]

_____. In the mid-twentieth century, several important   [owners of businesses]

studies of inequality in American communities revealed the existence of a

complex _____ system as well as a racial   [social-class]

_____ system.   [caste]

The shift from an economy based on manufacturing to one based on

services has resulted in a _____ of class lines and an   [blurring]

_____ of class conflict between industrial workers and   [easing]

the owners and managers of the means of production. Nevertheless, some

sociologists argue that Americans continue to recognize

_____ divisions. When people are asked what social   [social-class]

class they belong to, the largest proportions say that they are members of

the _____. They base their class assignments on   [middle class]

_____, which is derived primarily from   [socioeconomic status]

_____ but also takes into account   [occupation]

_____, _____, and   [family status; education]

_____.   [earned income]

Social-class position has important consequences for the daily life of

individuals and households. Members of the _____   [upper classes]

tend to have better health and more adequate health care than people in the

_____. They are also likely to receive more and better   [lower classes]

Harcourt Brace & Company.

_____. In politics, the poor members of the working [education]

class generally support the _____ party, while those in [Democratic]

the middle and upper classes support the _____ party. [Republican]

The _____ is estimated at about 4 percent of the U.S. [upper class]

population. The richest among them control 40 percent of all

_____ in the United States. This class may be divided [personal wealth]

into the wealthiest and more prestigious families, who make up the

_____ or "high society," and families who have [elite]

acquired their money more _____. Sociologists [recently]

continually debate whether the upper class in America is also the society's

_____. [ruling class]

Members of the upper-middle class tend to be _____. [highly educated

The middle class, the largest single class in American society, is culturally professionals]

extremely _____. In the past it was thought to be [diverse]

associated with a _____, _____, [family-oriented; conserv-

_____ lifestyle, but recent studies have shown that ative; suburban]

there is no easily identified middle-class suburban culture.

The _____ class, which accounts for at least one-third [working]

of the U.S. population, is undergoing rapid and difficult changes as

_____ change and [production technologies]

_____ spreads throughout the world. Members of this [industrialization]

class are employed in skilled, semiskilled, or unskilled

_____ occupations, and many are [manual]

_____. The American working class can be divided [union members]

into _____ workers and those employed in [industrial]

_____. There is more racial and ethnic [skilled crafts]

_____ in the working class than in other classes. [diversity]

Estimates of the proportion of the population living in poverty vary widely,

depending on the standard used to define poverty. According to official

statistics, _____ percent of Americans live in poverty. [14.5]

A significant proportion of the poor have _____ that [jobs]

do not pay enough to support their families. Another large percentage of

poor families are _____ families headed by [single-parent]

_____. Other categories of poor people include [women]

_____ people living on fixed incomes, marginally [aged]

Harcourt Brace & Company.

employed _____ and part-time miners, chronically   [rural workers]

unemployed _____, and   [manual workers]

_____ and their families. Another group of people in   [disabled workers]

danger of becoming poor are _____.   [farmers]

Policy debates on the issue of _____ are often clouded   [poverty]

by problems of definition. Although many Americans believe in equality of

_____, they are less committed to the ideal of equality   [opportunity]

of _____. Most sociologists agree that a completely   [result]

_____ society is impossible to achieve; instead, they   [egalitarian]

concentrate on the extent of _____ in American   [upward mobility]

society.

Research on _____ (from low   [long-distance upward

family status to membership in the elite) has revealed relatively high rates of   mobility]

mobility into _____ occupations by children of fathers   [elite]

in _____. Although this suggests that   [manual trades]

_____ is possible for everyone, in reality only a very   [long-distance mobility]

small number of people are able to achieve this dramatic form of upward

mobility.

In recent decades _____ has become an ever more   [educational attainment]

important route to a better career. Yet the benefits of education are highly

influenced by _____. It has been shown that   [social class]

_____ is the most important variable in the extent to   [family background]

which children succeed in school and the amount of education they

eventually receive—more important than individual

_____ or the _____ of the   [intelligence; quality]

schools children attend. Another trend that has affected the possibility of

social mobility in the United States is the large scale participation of

_____ in the labor force. It appears, however, that the   [women]

addition of a second paycheck does not add enough to the family's income

to raise the household to another _____.   [social class]

Matching Exercise

For each of the following terms, identify the correct definition and enter the appropriate letter in the blank in front of the definition.

Harcourt Brace & Company.

a.   educational attainment
b.   educational achievement
c.   occupational prestige
d.   ghetto
e.   socioeconomic status (SES)
f.   equality of opportunity
g.   equality of result
h.   long-distance upward mobility

_____1.   a section of a city that is segregated either racially or culturally.

_____2.   equality in the actual outcomes of people's attempts to improve their material well-being and prestige.

_____3.   mastery of basic reading, writing, and computational skills.

_____4.   a broad social-class ranking based on occupational status, family prestige, educational attainment, and earned income.

_____5.   a form of upward mobility in which a person rises within his or her own lifetime from low family status to membership in a professional or managerial elite.

_____6.   the number of years of school an individual has completed.

_____7.   the honor or prestige attributed to specific occupations by adults in a society.

_____8.   equal opportunity to achieve desired levels of material well-being and prestige.

Self-Test

_____1.   Which of the following is *not* a basic measure of inequality in any society?
a.   wealth   c.   educational attainment
b.   occupational prestige   d.   social class

_____2.   The Jeffersonian view of American society applied to
a.   the larger cities.   c.   farmers and town dwellers.
b.   the southern states.   d.   Native Americans.

_____3.   The Middletown study was conducted by
a.   Mary and Robert Jackman.
b.   Helen and Robert Lynd.
c.   William Lloyd Warner.
d.   St. Clair Drake and Horace Cayton.

_____4.   The Yankee City study showed that
a.   people combine notions of economic class with other dimensions to form a system of social-class rankings.
b.   American society does not have a well-defined social-class system.
c.   the United States is characterized by a complex caste system.
d.   blue-collar workers form a powerful class in American society, confirming the prediction made by Marx.

_____5.   Which of the following statements is true?
  a.   Few people have trouble assigning themselves to a social class.
  b.   Blacks and Hispanics are more likely than whites to assign themselves to the middle class.
  c.   Holders of jobs in skilled trades tend to be assigned to the working class.
  d.   The farm population in the United States constitutes a distinct social class.

_____6.   What percentage of the total population can be identified as the upper class?
  a.   10   c.   about 4
  b.   between 5 and 7   d.   0.5

_____7.   Highly educated professionals tend to identify themselves as members of the
  a.   upper class.   c.   upper-middle class.
  b.   professional class.   d.   upper-working class.

_____8.   People whose income is derived from small businesses form a segment of the
  a.   upper class.   c.   working class.
  b.   middle class.   d.   lower class.

_____9.   Which social class is undergoing the most rapid change in America today?
  a.   the upper class   c.   the working class
  b.   the middle class   d.   the poor

_____10.   The most diverse class in racial and ethnic terms is the
  a.   upper class.   c.   middle class.
  b.   upper-middle class.   d.   working class.

_____11.   Which of the following is a reason for the increase in poverty during the 1980s?
  a.   an increase in low-wage jobs
  b.   a narrowing gap between rich and poor
  c.   an increase in father-headed households
  d.   all of the above

_____12.   When people say that they believe in equality, they usually mean
  a.   equality of opportunity.   c.   gender equality.
  b.   equality of result.   d.   all of the above

_____13.   According to Herbert Gans, poverty has "positive" functions in that it
  a.   ensures that society's dirty work will be done.
  b.   forces people to work at low wages and thereby subsidize the upper classes.
  c.   creates jobs for people who serve the poor or protect the rest of society from them.
  d.   all of the above

_____14.   In sociological terms, the theme of "rags-to-riches" stories is
  a.   the role of family background in social mobility.
  b.   the possibility of long-distance upward mobility.
  c.   the myth of equality of opportunity.
  d.   the need for intentional redistribution of income.

_____15.   The addition of a second paycheck to a family's income usually
  a.   raises the family to a higher social class.
  b.   allows the family to maintain its existing class position.
  c.   results in downward mobility because of the tax structure.
  d.   causes the wife's social class to differ from the husband's.

Harcourt Brace & Company.

T/F   16.   The distribution of wealth and income is more equal than that of educational attainment and occupational prestige.

T/F   17.   The Middletown study found little hostility among economic classes.

T/F   18.   Drake and Cayton demonstrated the existence of a racial caste system in large northern cities.

T/F   19.   A research method that assigns people to social classes on the basis of interviews with residents of their community is known as the objective method.

T/F   20.   Most differences in educational attainment are explained by the pressure placed on children by upper-middle-class parents.

21.   How has the shift from an economy based on manufacturing to one based on services affected the class structure of American society?

_____

_____

_____

_____

22.   Briefly describe each of the main social classes in the United States today, including its estimated size as a percentage of the total population.

The upper classes:_____

_____

The middle classes:_____

_____

The working class:_____

_____

The poor:_____

_____

23.   Structural transformations in the U.S. economy are changing the patterns of class stratification that have existed since early in this century. What are some of those changes, and how are they affecting different social classes?

_____

_____

_____

24.   It used to be considered reasonable for a woman's social-class position to be measured either by that of her father or by that of her husband. Is this a reasonable assumption today? Why or why not?

_____

_____

_____

_____

25.   Briefly describe some of the ways in which social class affects life chances.

_____

_____

_____

_____

CHAPTER 13 Inequalities of Race and Ethnicity

The Meaning of Race and Ethnicity
    Race: A Social Concept
    Racism
    Ethnic Groups and Minorities

When Worlds Collide: Patterns of Intergroup Relations
    Genocide
    Expulsion
    Slavery
    Segregation
    Assimilation

Culture and Intergroup Relations
    Stereotypes
    Prejudice and Discrimination
    Ethnic and Racial Nationalism
    Affirmative Action

Theories of Racial and Ethnic Inequality
    Social–Psychological Theories
    Interactionist Theories
    Functionalist Theories
    Conflict Theories
    Ecological Theories

A Piece of the Pie

Research Frontiers: The Growing Hispanic Presence in North America

---

Objectives

1. To become familiar with the sociological concepts of race and ethnicity.
2. To understand how biological concepts of race, when linked to cultural biases, can produce dangerous ideologies.
3. To appreciate the fact that ethnic groups are characterized by a sense of "peoplehood."
4. To be able to discuss the main types of intergroup relations that have marked societies throughout history, from genocide to assimilation.
5. To become familiar with the cultural dimensions of intergroup relations, particularly stereotypes and prejudice.
6. To be able to discuss the functionalist, interactionist, and conflict approaches to intergroup relations.

Harcourt Brace & Company.

Review

To test your comprehension of the material in the chapter, cover the words in the margin with a sheet of paper and fill in the blanks in the following summary. It is not always necessary to use exactly the same words as those in the margin.

In biology, the term _____ refers to an inbreeding   [race]
population that develops distinctive physical characteristics that are
hereditary. However, the choice of physical characteristics to consider in
classifying people into races is _____, and human   [arbitrary]
groups have exchanged their genes through mating to such an extent that it
is impossible to identify _____.   ["pure" races]
The _____ concept of race has emerged from the   [social]
interactions of various populations over long periods of human history. It
varies from one society to another, depending on how the people of that
society feel about the importance of certain _____   [physical]
differences among human beings. Racism is an
_____ based on the belief that an observable,   [ideology]
supposedly inherited trait is a mark of _____ that   [inferiority]
justifies _____ treatment of people with that trait.   [discriminatory]
_____ are populations that have a sense of group   [Ethnic groups]
identity based on a distinctive cultural pattern and shared ancestry. They
usually have a sense of "_____" that is maintained   [peoplehood]
within a larger society. Ethnic and racial populations are often treated as
_____—people who, because of their physical or   [minority groups]
cultural characteristics, are singled out from others in the society for
differential and unequal treatment.
Intergroup relations can be placed along a continuum ranging from
_____ to _____, or from   [intolerance; tolerance]
genocide to assimilation. _____ is the intentional   [Genocide]
extermination of one population, defined as a "race" or a "people," by a
more dominant population. It is almost always justified by the belief that the
people who are being exterminated are _____.   [less than human]
_____ is the forcible removal of one population   [Expulsion]
from territory claimed by another population. It has taken a variety of forms
in American history, including the expulsion of

_____ from their ancestral lands, the   [Native Americans]

_____ movement of the nineteenth century, and the   [oriental exclusion]

detention of _____ during World War II.   [Japanese Americans]

_____ is the ownership of a population—defined by   [Slavery]

racial, ethnic, or political criteria—by another population that has complete

control over the enslaved population. It has been called "the

_____ institution" because it has existed in some of   [peculiar]

the world's greatest civilizations, including the United States.

Although African-American slaves gained their freedom during the Civil

War, a long period of _____ followed. This term   [segregation]

refers to the ecological and institutional separation of races or ethnic groups.

It may be either _____ or   [voluntary]

_____. Involuntary segregation may be either   [involuntary]

_____ (created by laws that prohibit certain groups   [_de jure_]

from interacting with others) or _____ (created by   [_de facto_]

unwritten norms).

_____ is the pattern of intergroup relations in which   [Assimilation]

a minority group is forced or encouraged or voluntarily seeks to blend into

the majority population and eventually disappears as a

_____ people within the larger society. In the United   [distinct]

States, three views of assimilation have prevailed since the early nineteenth

century. They are "_____," the demand that   [Anglo-conformity]

culturally distinct groups give up their own cultures and adopt the dominant

Anglo-Saxon culture; "_____," the theory that there   [the melting pot]

would be a social and biological merging of ethnic and racial groups; and

"_____," the belief that culturally distinct groups can   [cultural pluralism]

retain their communities and much of their culture and still be integrated into

American society.

_____ are inflexible images of a racial or cultural   [Stereotypes]

group that are held without regard to whether or not they are true. They are

often associated with _____, an attitude that   [prejudice]

prejudges a person, either positively or negatively, on the basis of

characteristics of a group of which that person is a member.

_____ refers to actual behavior that treats people   [Discrimination]

unfairly on the basis of their group membership;

Harcourt Brace & Company.

_____ is the systematic exclusion of people from equal participation in a particular social institution because of their race, religion, or ethnicity. Social movements whose purpose is to oppose institutional discrimination are often supported by [institutional discrimination]

_____, the belief that one's ethnic group constitutes a distinct people whose culture is and should be separate from that of the larger society. Policies designed to correct persistent racial and ethnic inequalities in promotion, hiring, and access to other opportunities are referred to as _____. [ethnic nationalism]

[affirmative action]

Social–psychological theories of ethnic and racial inequality hold that a society's patterns of discrimination stem from _____ [individual] psychological orientations toward members of _____. [out-groups]

_____ explanations go beyond the individual level to [Interactionist] see how hostility or sympathy toward other groups is produced by the norms of interaction that evolve within and between groups. The

_____ perspective generally seeks patterns of social [functionalist] integration that help maintain stability in a society.

_____ theories trace the origins of racial and ethnic [Conflict] inequality to the conflict between classes in capitalist societies. The conflict perspective includes the theory of _____, which [internal colonialism] holds that many minority groups are essentially colonial peoples within the larger society. Finally, _____ theories of race [ecological] relations explore the processes by which conflict between racial or ethnic groups develops and is resolved.

The persistence of racial inequality in the United States is a source of continuing controversy. This complex problem is a result of a number of factors besides racial prejudice and discrimination. Other factors are high rates of _____ and the effects of [family breakup] _____ changes in the American economy. Although [structural] social mobility is more available to blacks today that it was before the civil rights movement, the majority of blacks are in insecure _____ [working-class] jobs or are _____. [unemployed]

Harcourt Brace & Company.

Matching Exercise

For each of the following terms, identify the correct definition and enter the appropriate letter in the blank in front of the definition.

a. race
b. racism
c. ethnic group
d. minority group
e. genocide
f. expulsion
g. slavery
h. segregation
i. *de jure* segregation
j. *de facto* segregation
k. Jim Crow

l. assimilation
m. ethnic stratification
n. pluralistic society
o. stereotype
p. prejudice
q. discrimination
r. institutional discrimination
s. ethnic nationalism
t. scapegoat
u. projection
v. internal colonialism

_____1.   the intentional extermination of one population by a more dominant population.

_____2.   an inflexible image of the members of a particular group that is held without regard to whether or not it is true.

_____3.   a population that, because of its members' physical or cultural characteristics, is singled out from others in the society for differential and unequal treatment.

_____4.   a pattern of intergroup relations in which a minority group is absorbed into the majority population and eventually disappears as a distinct group.

_____5.   segregation that is created by formal legal sanctions that prohibit certain groups from interacting with others or that place limits on such interactions.

_____6.   a convenient target for hostility.

_____7.   the ownership of one racial, ethnic, or politically determined group by another group that has complete control over the enslaved group.

_____8.   a society in which different ethnic and racial groups are able to maintain their own cultures and lifestyles while gaining equality in the institutions of the larger society.

_____9.   an inbreeding population that develops distinctive physical characteristics that are hereditary.

_____10.   an attitude that prejudges a person on the basis of a real or imagined characteristic of a group of which that person is a member.

_____11.   a theory of racial and ethnic inequality that suggests that some minorities are essentially colonial peoples within the larger society.

_____12.   the system of formal and informal segregation that existed in the United States from the late 1860s to the early 1970s.

_____13.   the belief that one's own ethnic group constitutes a distinct people whose culture is and should be separate from that of the larger society.

_____14.   a population that has a sense of group identity based on shared ancestry and distinctive cultural patterns.

_____15.   behavior that treats people unfairly on the basis of their group membership.

_____16.   an ideology based on the belief that an observable, supposedly inherited trait is a mark of inferiority that justifies discriminatory treatment of people with that trait.

_____17.   the ranking of ethnic groups in a social hierarchy on the basis of each group's similarity to the dominant group.

_____18.   the psychological process whereby we attribute to other people behaviors and attitudes that we are unwilling to accept in ourselves.

_____19.   the ecological and institutional separation of races or ethnic groups.

_____20.   the systematic exclusion of people from equal participation in a particular institution because of their group membership.

_____21.   the forcible removal of one population from a territory claimed by another population.

_____22.   segregation that is created and maintained by unwritten norms.

Self-Test

_____1.   In biology, an inbreeding human population that develops distinctive physical characteristics that are hereditary is
    a.   an ethnic group.   c.   a minority group.
    b.   a race.   d.   none of the above

_____2.   The ideology of racism is based on which of the following beliefs?
    a.   One racial group is biologically superior to another.
    b.   Members of different racial groups have different personalities.
    c.   Ethical standards differ from one racial group to another.
    d.   all of the above

_____3.   According to the definitions given in the text, women can be viewed as
    a.   a racial group.   c.   a minority group.
    b.   an ethnic group.   d.   none of the above

_____4.   The elimination of the Hottentots from Africa by the British and Dutch during the nineteenth century is an example of
    a.   genocide.   c.   segregation.
    b.   expulsion.   d.   assimilation.

_____5.   The forced detention of Japanese Americans during World War II is an example of
    a.   genocide.   c.   slavery.
    b.   expulsion.   d.   segregation.

Harcourt Brace & Company.

_____ 6.   The phrase "the peculiar institution" has been used to describe which of the following?
a.   genocide   c.   slavery
b.   expulsion   d.   segregation

_____ 7.   Segregation that results from the desire of a people to live separately and maintain its own culture and institutions is known as
a.   *de jure* segregation.   c.   voluntary segregation.
b.   *de facto* segregation.   d.   institutional segregation.

_____ 8.   The Jim Crow system that governed race relations in the United States from the Civil War until the early 1970s was a form of
a.   *de jure* segregation.   c.   voluntary segregation.
b.   *de facto* segregation.   d.   assimilation.

_____ 9.   In Brazil people recognize at least fifteen racial types, but racial discrimination is largely absent. This is an example of
a.   *de jure* segregation.   c.   assimilation.
b.   *de facto* segregation.   d.   Anglo-conformity.

_____ 10.   The theory that there would be a cultural and biological merger of racial and ethnic groups in the United States became known as
a.   the crucible.   c.   Anglo-conformity.
b.   the melting pot.   d.   ethnic stratification.

_____ 11.   Switzerland, whose population includes three cultural groups that participate equally in the society's institutions, is an example of
a.   ethnic stratification.   c.   ethnic nationalism.
b.   the melting pot.   d.   cultural pluralism.

_____ 12.   The notion that all Indians walk single file is an example of
a.   ethnic nationalism.   c.   projection.
b.   institutional discrimination.   d.   a stereotype.

_____ 13.   The black-power movement is an example of
a.   ethnic nationalism.   c.   cultural pluralism.
b.   reverse discrimination.   d.   projection.

_____ 14.   The process whereby we attribute to other people behaviors and feelings that we are unable to accept in ourselves is known as
a.   frustration–aggression.   c.   authoritarianism.
b.   projection.   d.   scapegoating.

_____ 15.   The severity of social problems among African Americans has been associated with
a.   greater exposure to prejudice and discrimination.
b.   higher rates of family breakup.
c.   the effects of structural changes in the economy.
d.   all of the above

T/F   16.   The black, white, and oriental races are a set of distinct populations based on biological differences.

T/F   17.   A minority group need not constitute a numerical minority of the society's population.

T/F   18.   The apartheid system that until recently was protected by law in South Africa is an example of de facto segregation.

T/F   19.   American society is characterized by a fully developed cultural pluralism.

T/F   20.   Social interaction between groups tends to reinforce in-group, out-group barriers.

21.   Describe the five main patterns of intergroup relations and give an example of each.

Genocide:_____

_____

Expulsion:_____

_____

Slavery:_____

_____

Segregation:_____

_____

Assimilation:_____

_____

22.   What is Martin Kilson's argument in favor of affirmative action? Why might a conservative African American, such as Justice Clarence Thomas, argue against affirmative action?

_____

_____

_____

_____

23.   Briefly describe Robert Park's cyclical model of intergroup relations in modern cities. Give an example of the operation of these processes.

_____

_____

_____

_____

24.   Look at the vignette at the beginning of the chapter and explain what Polly Heidleberg meant by "higher ground." Describe some aspects of the social movement that were required in order to reach that "higher ground."

_____

_____

_____

_____

25.   What do we mean when we say that among all the major Hispanic groups in the United States, Puerto Ricans most share the structural conditions that African Americans encounter?

_____

_____

_____

_____

CHAPTER 14   Inequalities of Gender

Gender and Inequality
>Patterns of Gender Inequality

Sex Versus Gender
>Gender Socialization and Gender Separation
>Problems With the Gender Separation Theory
>Gender and Sexuality

Gender Stratification
>Gender Roles: A Cultural Phenomenon
>Historical Patterns of Gender Stratification

Gender Inequality in Industrial Societies
>The Gender-Poverty Ratio
>Sexism

The Women's Movement

Women at Work
>The Second Shift

Research Frontiers: Women in the Developing World

Objectives

1. To be able to differentiate between sex and gender and apply this distinction to debates about gender inequality.
2. To understand the nature of gender socialization—that is, the patterns of interaction that produce masculine and feminine roles and the attitudes that support these roles.
3. To understand how gender roles have changed throughout history.
4. To explore the origins of sexism and homophobia and see how these behaviors injure those against whom they are directed.
5. To see patriarchy, gender inequality, and underdevelopment as global issues that have stimulated efforts to empower women in an attempt to change the course of social and economic development.

Review

To test your comprehension of the material in the chapter, cover the words in the margin with a sheet of paper and fill in the blanks in the following summary. It is not always necessary to use exactly the same words as those in the margin.

_____ refers to the biological differences between males   [Sex]

and females, including the _____ sex characteristics that   [primary]

are present at birth and the _____ sex characteristics that   [secondary]

Harcourt Brace & Company.

develop later. Some people are born as _____; their   [hermaphrodites]
primary sexual organs have features of both male and female organs,
making it difficult to categorize the person as male or female. Another
ambiguous sexual category consists of _____, who feel   [transsexuals]
very strongly that the sexual organs they were born with do not conform to
their deep-seated sense of what their sex should be.

_____ refers to the culturally defined ways of acting as a   [Gender]
male or a female that become part of an individual's personal sense of self.
Gender socialization in the family and in schools tends to separate males and
females into different _____ with their own forms of   [social worlds]
activity and language. However, boys and girls are increasingly
participating in the same types of activities in their schools and
communities, and many parents, teachers, and administrators seek to avoid
the worst effects of gender _____.   [separation]

_____ refers to the manner in which a person engages in   [Sexuality]
the intimate behaviors connected with genital stimulation, orgasm, and
procreation. It is profoundly influenced by _____ and   [cultural norms]
_____ like the family and the school, as well as by   [social institutions]
_____ like the class system of a society. Universal   [social structures]
cultural norms exerting social control over sexuality include the
_____, _____, and   [incest taboo; marriage]
_____, but even these norms include variations and   [heterosexuality]
differing degrees of sanction. _____ refers to sexual   [Heterosexuality]
orientation toward the opposite sex, in contrast to _____,   [homosexuality]
or sexual orientation toward the same sex, and _____, or   [bisexuality]
sexual orientation toward either sex. Norms of heterosexuality function to
ensure that there is _____ between men and women   [genital sexual inter-
in the interest of population replacement and growth. Fear of homosexuals   course]
and same-sex attraction is known as _____.   [homophobia]
All human societies are stratified by gender, meaning that males and females
are channeled into specific _____ and   [statuses]
_____. Until quite recently it was assumed that there   [roles]
were two separate spheres of life for men and women. Out of this gender-
based division of labor grew the notion of differences in men's and
women's _____ and _____. These   [abilities; personalities]

differences were thought to be based on biological and psychological differences between males and females. In the twentieth century, however, evidence from the social sciences has established that gender roles are not innate but are strongly influenced by _____.   [culture]
Preindustrial societies are usually rigidly _____. As   [sex-segregated]
societies increase in size and complexity, women usually become

_____ to men. The origins of gender inequality in most   [subordinated]
modern societies can be traced to their _____ periods. In   [feudal]
Europe, for example, the norms of _____ specified that   [courtly love]
women do not engage in warfare or politics or compete with men in any sphere of life beyond those reserved for women.

In modern industrial societies boys and girls are socialized into

"_____" and "_____" roles. In their   [masculine; feminine]
adult years men enjoy more _____,   [wealth]
_____, and _____ than women do.   [prestige; leisure]
Gender _____ in modern societies is reflected in   [stratification]
attitudes that reinforce the subordinate status of women.

_____ refers to an ideology that justifies prejudice or   [Sexism]
discrimination based on sex.

The modern women's movement arose in the _____ out   [mid-1960s]
of an already existing network of women's organizations, together with a

less formal network of women in _____ groups. The   [consciousness-raising]
movement won significant victories during the _____   [1960s]
and _____ and began to change the way men and   [1970s]
women think about gender roles.

The most frequently cited problems of women in the workplace are low

_____, differentials in _____,   [wages; fringe benefits]
"_____" jobs, sexual _____, lack of   [dead end; harassment]
_____, stress over _____ roles, and   [child care; multiple]
lack of _____ time. Another problem is the segregation   [leisure]
of women into the "pink-collar ghettos" of _____ and   [secretarial]
_____ work. Women who work outside the home are   [clerical]
also expected to perform the bulk of domestic and child care work. This

"_____" is an example of the persistence of   [second shift]
_____, the dominance of men over women.   [patriarchy]

Harcourt Brace & Company.

Matching Exercise

For each of the following terms, identify the correct definition and enter the appropriate letter in the blank in front of the definition.

a. sex
b. hermaphrodite
c. transsexuals
d. gender
e. sexuality
f. heterosexuality
g. homosexuality
h. bisexuality
i. gender role
j. sexism
k. patriarchy

_____1.   the culturally defined ways of acting as a male or a female that become part of an individual's personal sense of self.

_____2.   an ideology that justifies prejudice and discrimination based on sex.

_____3.   sexual orientation toward the opposite sex.

_____4.   a person whose primary sexual organs have features of both male and female organs, making it difficult to categorize the individual as male or female.

_____5.   the biological differences between males and females, including the primary sex characteristics that are present at birth (i.e., the presence of specific male or female genitalia) and the secondary sex characteristics that develop later (facial and body hair, voice quality, etc.).

_____6.   sexual orientation toward either sex.

_____7.   the manner in which a person engages in the intimate behaviors connected with genital stimulation, orgasm, and procreation.

_____8.   the dominance of men over women.

_____9.   people who feel very strongly that the sexual organs they were born with do not conform to their deep-seated sense of what their sex should be.

_____10.   a set of behaviors considered appropriate for an individual of a particular gender.

_____11.   sexual orientation toward the same sex.

Self-Test

_____1.   People who feel that they were born with the "wrong" sexual organs are termed
    a.   transsexuals.   c.   bisexuals.
    b.   homosexuals.   d.   hermaphrodites.

_____2.   An individual's gender identity is a result of
           a.   biological sex.   c.   early socialization.
           b.   hospital procedures.   d.   parental preferences.

_____3.   Compared to boys' play groups, girls' groups are more likely to involve
           a.   complex structures and hierarchies of status.
           b.   arguments over rules.
           c.   turn taking and cooperation.
           d.   public protests to umpires or other adults.

_____4.   Which of the following is a universal cultural norm exerting social control over
           sexuality?
           a.   the incest taboo   c.   heterosexuality
           b.   marriage   d.   all of the above

_____5.   According to recent surveys, about _____ percent of U.S. men are exclusively
           homosexual.
           a.   1   c.   10
           b.   4   d.   14

_____6.   Stratification by gender is characteristic of
           a.   preindustrial societies.   c.   urban industrial societies.
           b.   feudal societies.   d.   all human societies.

_____7.   One of the first social scientists to conduct research on gender roles was
           a.   Sigmund Freud.   c.   Karl Marx.
           b.   Margaret Mead.   d.   Deborah Tannen.

_____8.   The division of labor by gender is
           a.   an outgrowth of the biological differences between the sexes.
           b.   similar in all human societies.
           c.   heavily influenced by culture.
           d.   determined by a society's level of technological development.

_____9.   Which of the following statements is true?
           a.   In preindustrial societies, wealth and power often play a greater role in
                social stratification than gender.
           b.   As societies increase in size and complexity, men usually become
                subordinated to women.
           c.   Industrial societies tend to be rigidly sex segregated.
           d.   None of the above.

_____10. Studies of gender inequality in industrial nations find that the gender-poverty ratio
           is highest in
           a.   the United States.   c.   Italy.
           b.   Sweden.   d.   France.

_____11. The objectification of women is an example of
           a.   a gender role.   c.   sexism.
           b.   sexuality.   d.   patriarchy.

Harcourt Brace & Company.

_____12.   Which of the following statements is *not* true?
      a.   Most observers of American society did not foresee the resurgence of the women's movement in the mid-1960s.
      b.   The modern women's movement developed out of an existing network of women's organizations.
      c.   The women's movement won significant victories during the 1970s.
      d.   Women now earn almost as much as men for the same types of work.

_____13.   What proportion of American women are currently in the labor force?
      a.   about one third
      b.   about half
      c.   about 70 percent
      d.   almost all women between the ages of 20 and 65

_____14.   What is meant by the "feminine mystique"?
      a.   The belief that women can find fulfillment only as wives and mothers.
      b.   The fact that women have higher life expectancies than men.
      c.   The segregation of women into secretarial and clerical jobs.
      d.   The fact that as more women enter an occupation, its average pay tends to decrease.

_____15.   Sociologist Arlie Hochschild coined the phrase "the second shift" to refer to
      a.   the expectation that women will leave their jobs to raise children and return after the children are grown.
      b.   the time women spend doing household chores after working at a job outside the home.
      c.   the fact that many women must work at two jobs to make ends meet.
      d.   the time devoted to household chores in dual-career families.

T/F   16.   Gender refers to the biological differences between men and women, including both primary and secondary sex characteristics.

T/F   17.   An important theme in social-scientific research is the way gender socialization tends to separate males and females into different social worlds.

T/F   18.   Heterosexuality is practiced in some form in all societies.

T/F   19.   As societies evolve from hunting and gathering to agrarian production, the division of labor by sex becomes less varied.

T/F   20.   The origins of gender inequality in most modern societies can be traced to feudal norms such as chivalry and courtly love.

21.   Describe the gender separation theory and give some arguments in support of it as well as some criticisms of it.

_____

_____

_____

_____

Harcourt Brace & Company.

22.   What evidence is there that gender roles are shaped by culture rather than by biological differences between the sexes?

_____

_____

_____

_____

23.   How does sexism contribute to overall patterns of stratification in the United States? What evidence can you marshal to show that it is a continuing problem?

_____

_____

_____

_____

24.   Briefly summarize the history of the modern women's movement. What is the status of the movement today?

_____

_____

_____

_____

25.   Present evidence demonstrating that patriarchy persists in the United States today.

_____

_____

_____

_____

CHAPTER 15   Inequalities of Youth and Age

Sources of Age Stratification
    The Life Course—Society's Age Structure
    Cohorts and Age Structures
    Life Expectancy
Age Stratification and Inequality
    The Challenge of Youth
    Age and Inequality
Social Movements Among the Elderly
    The Hospice Movement
Research Frontiers: Population Aging and Stewardship

Objectives

1. To be able to use population pyramids to demonstrate the effects of age cohorts passing through a population.
2. To trace the influence of the baby boom generation on social policy and social movements in the United States.
3. To appreciate the fact that age distinctions produce particular patterns of inequality and specific differences in the lives of people of different ages.
4. To understand how age influences patterns of stratification and how those patterns differ in different societies.
5. To understand the distinctions between biological and social age, and to see how changing views of the elderly have led to major shifts in the roles of elderly men and women.

Review

To test your comprehension of the material in the chapter, cover the words in the margin with a sheet of paper and fill in the blanks in the following summary. It is not always necessary to use exactly the same words as those in the margin.

In many societies _____ determines a great deal about   [age]

the opportunities open to a person and what kind of life that person leads.

The study of aging and the elderly is termed _____. All   [gerontology]

societies channel people into _____, or sets of statuses   [age grades]

and roles based on age. The transitions among these age grades create a

_____ and are often marked by ceremonies known as   [life course]

_____.   [rites of passage]

_____ are people of about the same age who are passing   [Age cohorts]

through life's stages together. The "_____" cohorts,   [baby boom]

which were produced by rapid increases in the birthrate from about 1945

through the early 1960s, have profoundly influenced American society. A

sizable proportion of the children of the baby boom generation are members

of _____ groups.   [minority]

By _____ we mean the average number of years a   [life expectancy]

member of a given population can expect to live beyond his or her present

age. As life expectancy in a population increases, the proportion of the

population that is _____ also increases.   [dependent on the adult

In urban industrial societies there are distinct patterns of   cohorts]

_____ in which age defines the roles one plays and the   [stratification]

rewards one can expect. The forces of _____ unleashed   [social change]

by colonialism, industrialization, urbanization, and population growth have

tended to disrupt the formal _____ systems of smaller,   [age grade]

more isolated societies.

Social definitions of _____ differ immensely throughout   [childhood]

the industrial world as well as between modern and traditional societies. As

a result of increasing incomes and the passage of child labor laws, children

became economically "_____" but emotionally   [worthless]

"_____." However, there is a growing gap between   [priceless]

"priceless" children and children who bear a heavy burden of

_____ and _____.   [poverty; deprivation]

At the turn of the century the largest segment of the U.S. population living

in poverty or near-poverty conditions was the _____. As   [elderly]

a result of programs such as Social Security and Medicare, rates of poverty

among the elderly have _____ dramatically. However,   [decreased]

the situation is not nearly so positive for elderly members of

_____ groups. As people age, they experience more   [minority]

medical problems and _____, but this does not mean that   [disabilities]

they must inevitably withdraw from social life. Social scientists who study

the situation of the elderly point out that longer lifespans need to be

accompanied by new concepts of _____ in more   [social roles]

advanced years.

_____ is an ideology that justifies prejudice or   [Ageism]

Harcourt Brace & Company.

discrimination based on age. As the proportion of older people in a society increases, as is occurring in the United States and Europe, the prevalence of ageism also increases.

As the population as a whole has aged, the impact of the elderly on American society has increased, and the way sociologists view old age has changed. Before the 1970s the most popular social-scientific view of aging was _____, the belief that as people grow older they   [disengagement theory] gradually "disengage" from their earlier roles. An alternative view of the elderly, known as _____, states that the elderly need   [activity theory] activities that will serve as outlets for their creativity and energy. Today gerontologists tend to reject both of these theories, seeing older people demanding opportunities to lead their lives in a variety of ways based on

_____.   [individual habits and

The growing proportion of elderly people in the population has led to   preferences] increased concern about the _____ of the elderly and   [quality of life] about death and the dying process. One outcome of this concern is the _____ movement, which attempts to provide dying   [hospice] people and their loved ones with a comfortable, dignified alternative to hospital death.

Matching Exercise

For each of the following terms, identify the correct definition and enter the appropriate letter in the blank in front of the definition.

a. gerontology
b. age grade
c. life course
d. rite of passage
e. age cohort
f. life expectancy
g. psychosocial risk behaviors
h. lifetime negative experiences
i. ageism

_____1.   a set of people of about the same age who are passing through the life course together.

_____2.   the average number of years a member of a given population can expect to live.

_____3.   the study of aging and older people.

_____4.   experiences that cause long-term stress, such as the death of a child or spouse.

_____5.   a ceremony marking the transition to a new stage of a culturally defined life course.

_____6.   a set of statuses and roles based on age.

_____7.   an ideology that justifies prejudice and discrimination based on age.

_____8.   a pathway along an age-differentiated, socially created sequence of transitions.

_____9.   behaviors that are detrimental to health, such as smoking and heavy drinking.

Self-Test

_____1.   Gerontology is the study of
    a.   statuses and roles based on age.
    b.   aging and the elderly.
    c.   sources of age stratification.
    d.   prejudice and discrimination based on age.

_____2.   Sets of statuses and roles based on age are
    a.   age grades.   c.   age ratios.
    b.   age cohorts.   d.   age categories.

_____3.   In Western civilization the concept of childhood as a phase of life
    a.   developed in the late seventeenth century.
    b.   did not appear until the passage of child labor laws.
    c.   until recently was applied only to girls.
    d.   is limited to the upper classes.

_____4.   The large base of a typical Third World population pyramid is caused by
    a.   high mortality rates in later cohorts.   c.   high birthrates.
    b.   high rates of infant mortality.   d.   all of the above.

_____5.   Demographers believe that in the next century the U.S. population will
    a.   continue to go through "boom" and "bust" cycles.
    b.   increase at a more rapid rate than in the past.
    c.   include a disproportionate number of very young children.
    d.   include increasing numbers of elderly people.

_____6.   At age 65 and beyond, more than 50 percent of North American women
    a.   have never married.   c.   have remarried.
    b.   are divorced.   d.   are widowed.

_____7.   The "age of majority" is
    a.   clearly defined by law.
    b.   generally considered to be the age at which one can vote.
    c.   the age at which one obtains a driver's license.
    d.   none of the above.

_____8.   During the nineteenth century, children were
       a.   more highly valued than they are today.
       b.   considered an economic liability.
       c.   often required to work for wages.
       d.   nurtured and protected longer than they are today.

_____9.   The most important indicator of the relative well-being of a nation's people is the
       a.   infant mortality rate.
       b.   rate of out-of-wedlock births.
       c.   percentage of low-birth weight babies.
       d.   rate of premature births.

_____10.   What proportion of the elderly are living in poverty?
       a.   5 percent   c.   40 percent
       b.   12 percent   d.   about half

_____11.   Which of the following often leads to poor health in old age?
       a.   psychosocial risk factors
       b.   lifetime negative experiences
       c.   lack of regular medical care
       d.   all of the above

_____12.   Research on sexual behavior among the elderly has found that
       a.   people lose their sexual potency after middle age.
       b.   elderly men are more interested in sex than women of the same age.
       c.   elderly people can no longer enjoy sex.
       d.   none of the above.

_____13.   According to Matilda White Riley and John W. Riley, Jr., there is an urgent need
       for
       a.   more retirement communities in which elderly people are free to disengage
             from social involvement at their own pace.
       b.   greater pressure on family members or close relatives to take responsibility
             for the care of the elderly.
       c.   small-scale programs that create work and volunteer opportunities for older
             people.
       d.   a broad-based campaign against ageism in American society.

_____14.   In general, gerontologists today believe that
       a.   older people willingly withdraw from their earlier roles.
       b.   the elderly need activities that will serve as outlets for their creativity and
             energy.
       c.   older people need to lead their lives in a variety of ways based on individual
             habits.
       d.   none of the above.

_____15.   The purpose of a hospice is to
       a.   make the dying patient as comfortable as possible.
       b.   prolong the patient's life.
       c.   reduce medical costs by treating the patient at home.
       d.   all of the above.

T/F   16.   All societies have cultural norms that divide the human life span into a series of
       predictable stages.

T/F   17.   The life expectancy of males is at least seven years longer than that of females.

T/F   18.   The forces of social change tend to disrupt the formal age grade systems of smaller, more isolated societies.

T/F   19.   As the proportion of older people in a society increases, the prevalence of ageism decreases.

T/F   20.   The living-dying interval refers to the experience of living with a major disability in one's last years.

21.   List the "seasons of life" that are characteristic of Western societies. Name the rites of passage that mark the transitions from one period of life to the next.

_____

_____

_____

_____

22.   Over half of all women over 65 are widows, whereas only 14 percent of men over age 65 are widowed. What factors account for these statistics?

_____

_____

_____

_____

23.   Compare the patterns of age stratification found in urban industrial societies and traditional agrarian or pastoral societies.

_____

_____

_____

24.   What changes have occurred in the condition of the elderly in the United States during the twentieth century?

_____

_____

_____

25.   Describe some examples of ageism that you have observed in your everyday life.

_____

_____

_____

_____

Harcourt Brace & Company.

CHAPTER 16   The Family

The Nature of Families
The Family as an Institution
Defining the Family
Variations in Family Structure
The Changing Family
The Family Life Cycle
Parenting, Stepparenting, and Social Change

Dynamics of Mate Selection and Marriage
Marriage as Exchange
Norms of Mate Selection
Romantic Love
Marriage and Divorce
Gay and Lesbian Relationships
Sources of Marital Instability
The Impact of Divorce

Perspectives on the Family
The Interactionist Perspective
The Conflict Perspective
Functionalist Views of the Family

Research Frontiers: The Black Family

Objectives

1. To appreciate the central place of the family as an institution in all human societies.
2. To be able to discuss the variety of family structures, using the concepts of kinship and the family life cycle.
3. To be able to discuss various theories that attempt to explain the process of mate selection.
4. To appreciate the role of homogamy in mate selection.
5. To understand the correlates of divorce and the impact of divorce and remarriage on the family.
6. To be able to apply the basic sociological perspectives to changes in the family in modern societies.

Review

To test your comprehension of the material in the chapter, cover the words in the margin with a sheet of paper and fill in the blanks in the following summary. It is not always necessary to use exactly the same words as those in the margin.

In all known societies almost everyone is socialized within a network of

family rights and obligations that are known as _____.   [family role relations]

In simple societies the family performs a large number of other functions as well, but in modern societies most of the functions that were traditionally performed by the family are performed partly or entirely by other

_____.   [social institutions]

A _____ is a group of people related by blood, marriage,   [family]
or adoption. Role relations among family members are known as

_____. The smallest unit of family structure is the   [kinship]

_____, consisting of two or more people related by   [nuclear family]
consanguineous ties or by adoption who share a household. The nuclear
family in which one is born and socialized is one's

_____, and the nuclear family one forms through   [family of orientation]

marriage or cohabitation is one's _____. An   [family of procreation]

_____ includes an individual's nuclear family plus all the [extended family]
nuclear families of his or her blood relatives.

The traditional household consisting of two parents and their children is no

longer the _____ American family. Since the 1940s there   [typical]

has been a dramatic increase in _____ single-parent   [female-headed]

families and in _____ households, as well as in the   [nonfamily]
numbers of women and men living alone and in the number of

_____, _____ couples.   [unmarried; same-sex]

Studies of changes in family structure have shown that family units become

_____ as societies undergo industrialization. Economic   [simpler]
and technological changes require the family to adapt to an economy in

which income is earned _____ the family; this means that   [outside]

families must become _____, more   [smaller]

_____, and more _____. More recent   [mobile; flexible]

research has found that _____ families have not entirely   [nuclear]

replaced _____ families, although extended families do   [extended]
not always live under one roof. Modern technologies such as the telephone
and the automobile enable members of smaller family units to maintain

_____ ties with their extended families.   [kinship]

The typical stages of the family life cycle are family

_____, start of _____, end of   [formation; childbearing]

_____, "_____," and family   [childbearing; empty nest]

_____ (that is, the death of one spouse). As it passes   [dissolution] through this cycle, every family experiences changes in its system of

_____. These changes present major   [role relations]

_____ challenges, which are often complicated by   [emotional]

divorce, remarriage, and the combining of children of different marriages in

_____.   [stepfamilies]

In all cultures the process of mate selection is carried out according to basic

rules of _____ and _____. In many   [bargaining; exchange]

societies the customary pattern of mate selection is the

"_____" marriage, in which the families of the bride and   [arranged]

groom negotiate the marriage contract. All cultures also have norms that

specify whether a person brought up in that culture may marry within or

outside the cultural group. Marriage within the group is termed

_____; marriage outside the group is termed   [endogamy]

_____. In societies in which marriages are based on   [exogamy]

attraction and love, individuals tend to marry people similar to themselves in

social background, a tendency that is referred to as

_____. This tendency generally serves to reproduce the   [homogamy]

society's system of _____ in the next generation and   [stratification]

maintains the separateness of _____ and   [religious]

_____ groups.   [racial]

Compared with the mate selection systems of other cultures, that of the

United States gives _____ greater prominence. Yet from   [love]

a scientific standpoint little is known about this complex emotional state. It

appears that people who fall in love tend to be alike in

_____ characteristics but different in their   [social]

_____ needs; however, this is not always the case. There   [psychological]

is also considerable evidence that love relationships are more lasting when

the partners' affection for each other is _____.   [roughly equal]

In the United States and other Western societies, the rate of

_____ has risen sharply since World War II. In the   [divorce]

1980s it was widely believed that the practice of _____   [cohabitation before

would result in greater marital stability, but in fact the divorce rate among   marriage]

couples who had lived together before marriage was actually

_____ than the rate for couples who had not done so.   [higher]

_____ has been found to be one of the leading factors in   [Age at marriage]

Harcourt Brace & Company.

divorce. Marriages that take place when the woman is in her

_____ or in her _____ are much more   [teens; thirties]

likely to end in divorce than marriages that take place when the woman is in

her _____. Among other factors that have been found to   [twenties]

be correlated with divorce are marked differences in the

_____ of the spouses, dependence on   [family backgrounds]

either spouse's _____,   [extended family]

_____ in either spouse's extended family, and early   [marital instability]

_____. Studies have found that the turmoil and stress of   [pregnancy]

divorce may last for _____ or more. Both men and   [a year]

women have a diminished capacity for _____ after   [parenting]

divorce and may come to depend on their _____ to help   [child]

them cope with the demands of their own lives.

The _____ context within which family life occurs can   [structural]

affect family interactions in a variety of ways. Problems may arise in

connection with the demands placed on the family by

_____ of the larger society or as a result of its position in   [institutions]

the society's _____. A basic contradiction that is inherent   [stratification system]

in the institution of the family is the need to maintain the

_____ of each member while providing love and support   [individuality]

for him or her within a set of _____ relationships.   [interdependent]

From a _____ perspective, changes in the family as an   [conflict]

institution cannot occur without _____ both within the   [conflict]

family and between the family and other institutions. Such conflict is

illustrated by public debates over family policies and

"_____."   [family values]

_____ theorists have called attention to the loss of family   [Functionalist]

functions that occurs as other social institutions assume functions that were

previously reserved for the family. At the same time, they note that modern

families play a vital part in early childhood _____, in the   [socialization]

_____ lives of their members, and in preparing older   [emotional]

children for _____.   [adult roles]

Matching Exercise

For each of the following terms, identify the correct definition and enter the appropriate letter in the blank in front of the definition.

a. family
b. kinship
c. nuclear family
d. family of orientation
e. family of procreation
f. extended family
g. endogamy
h. exogamy
i. homogamy

_____1.   a norm specifying that a person brought up in a particular culture may marry within the cultural group.

_____2.   the role relations among people who consider themselves to be related by blood, marriage, or adoption.

_____3.   the nuclear family a person forms through marriage or cohabitation.

_____4.   the tendency to marry a person who is similar to oneself in social background.

_____5.   an individual's nuclear family plus the nuclear families of his or her blood relatives.

_____6.   a group of people related by blood, marriage, or adoption.

_____7.   two or more people related by blood, marriage, or adoption.

_____8.   the nuclear family in which a person is born and raised.

_____9.   a norm specifying that a person brought up in a particular culture may marry outside the cultural group.

Self-Test

_____1.   In peasant and primitive societies the family typically
    a.   engages in warfare and feuds.
    b.   is submerged in the tribe or village social structure.
    c.   performs many of the tasks now performed by other social institutions.
    d.   is weakened by diseases and poverty.

_____2.   Which of the following is *not* an example of the family as a social institution?
    a.   paying for a child's education at a good college
    b.   teaching children moral values
    c.   a couple trying not to argue in front of the children
    d.   stepfamilies dealing with the logistics of holiday gatherings

_____3.   Which of the following is *not* a function of the family in modern societies?
a.   social control of reproduction
b.   socialization of new generations
c.   "social placement" of children in other institutions
d.   production of goods and services

_____4.   Two sisters and a niece living together would be an example of a
a.   traditional family.   c.   fictive family.
b.   nuclear family.   d.   reconstituted family.

_____5.   The family in which one is born and socialized is one's
a.   family of orientation.   c.   original family.
b.   family of procreation.   d.   extended family.

_____6.   According to William J. Goode, industrialization tends to favor the formation of
a.   extended families.   c.   conjugal families.
b.   single-parent families.   d.   none of the above

_____7.   In recent years the median age of Americans at first marriage has
a.   risen.   c.   fallen dramatically.
b.   decreased.   d.   remained the same.

_____8.   In all cultures the process of mate selection is carried out according to rules of
a.   endogamy.   c.   romantic love.
b.   exchange.   d.   complementary needs.

_____9.   Throughout the world, sociologists find that marriages tend toward
a.   exogamy.   c.   polygamy.
b.   endogamy.   d.   homogamy.

_____10.   Homogamy in mate selection tends to
a.   reproduce the society's stratification system in the next generation.
b.   maintain the separateness of religious groups.
c.   discourage interracial marriages.
d.   all of the above

_____11.   According to the theory of complementary needs, people who fall in love tend to differ in their
a.   education.   c.   psychological needs.
b.   income.   d.   family background.

_____12.   In recent years the divorce rate has
a.   accelerated dramatically.   c.   fallen rapidly.
b.   decreased slightly.   d.   remained the same.

_____13.   Which of the following has not been found to be correlated with marital instability and divorce?
a.   The couple met "on the rebound."
b.   The couple married after an engagement of less than three years.
c.   The family backgrounds of the spouses are markedly different.
d.   The wife became pregnant within the first year of marriage.

_____14. According to Cuber and Haroff, marriages in which the partners evolve elaborate ways of expressing hostility toward each other may be described as
   a.   conflict habituated.   c.   empty-shell marriages.
   b.   revitalized.   d.   all of the above

_____15. Which of the following statements is true?
   a.   The functionalist perspective views changes in family roles as resulting from changes in other institutions.
   b.   From the conflict perspective, changes in family roles result from conflict between the family and other institutions.
   c.   The interactionist perspective focuses on conflicts that occur within the family.
   d.   all of the above

T/F   16. A major function of the family is the "social placement" of children in the institutions of the larger society.

T/F   17. The nuclear family one forms through marriage or cohabitation is one's family of orientation.

T/F   18. In the 1960s and 1970s the proportion of married-couple families increased by about 20 percent.

T/F   19. Many social scientists believe that adolescence is a time for building interdependence.

T/F   20. Marriages have a higher probability of lasting when there is equality of roles within the household.

21. Identify the members of your nuclear family, your extended family, your family of orientation, and your family of procreation, if any. Are there any cases of exogamous marriage within your kinship network? How would divorce and remarriage alter this scheme?

_____

_____

_____

22. The text states that the stages of the family life cycle have become increasingly useful as indicators of change rather than as stages that all or most families can be expected to experience. Consider some families with which you are acquainted. Does this statement apply to them? If so, show how their experience differs from that of the "typical" or traditional family.

_____

_____

_____

23.   What was William J. Goode's theory about the family and industrialization? What evidence do sociologists now cite to show that this theory was overstated?

_____

_____

_____

_____

24.   Describe the "exchange theory" approach to mate selection and marriage. Can romantic attraction be explained by this theory? Can you think of an example in which exchange in mate selection might work against homogamy?

_____

_____

_____

_____

25.   How are changing patterns of labor force participation and changing attitudes about divorce and remarriage altering family roles? Broaden your discussion to the extended family network.

_____

_____

_____

_____

Harcourt Brace & Company.

CHAPTER 17 Religion

Religion in Society
Defining Religion
Religion as an Institution
The Power of Faith
Varieties of Religious Belief
Major World Religions
Classification of Religious Beliefs
Religion and Social Change
Structure and Change in Modern Religions
Forms of Religious Organization
Religious Interaction and Change
Trends in Religion in the United States
Unofficial Religion
Religiosity
Religious Pluralism
Fundamentalism
Research Frontiers: Social Change and the Catholic Church

Objectives

1. To be able to define religion and briefly trace its evolution.
2. To be able to describe and analyze religion, with emphasis on the spiritual and organizational aspects of religious institutions.
3. To recognize secularization as a trend that not only challenges religious institutions but also leads to an increase in the influence of other institutions.
4. To understand that secularization does not imply that religion will disappear from modern societies.
5. To be able to explain the Marx–Weber debate on the role of cultural institutions in social change.

Review

To test your comprehension of the material in the chapter, cover the words in the margin with a sheet of paper and fill in the blanks in the following summary. It is not always necessary to use exactly the same words as those in the margin.

_____ is among the oldest and most changeable and   [Religion]

complex of human social institutions. It has been defined as any set of

_____ answers to the dilemmas of human existence that   [coherent]

Harcourt Brace & Company.

makes the world _____. It has also been defined as a   [meaningful]

system of _____ and _____ that   [beliefs; rituals]

serves to bind people together into a social group. _____   [Rituals]

are formal patterns of activity that express a set of shared meanings; in the

case of religious rituals, the shared meanings are _____,   [sacred]

pertaining to phenomena that are regarded as extraordinary, transcendent,

and outside the everyday course of events.

Until comparatively recent times religion _____ the   [dominated]

cultural life of human societies. Since medieval times, however, the

traditional dominance of religion over other institutions has been reduced by

a process termed _____. This process is never complete;   [secularization]

religion continues to play an important role in the contemporary world.

In simpler and rather isolated societies, people may believe in a great force

or spirit, but they do not have a well-defined concept of God or a set of

rituals involving God. This form of religion is called

_____. More common among hunting and gathering   [simple supernaturalism]

societies is _____, in which all forms of life and all   [animism]

aspects of the earth are inhabited by gods or supernatural powers.

_____ belief systems, in contrast, usually conceive of a   [Theistic]

god or gods as separate from humans and from other living things on earth.

Many ancient religions were _____, meaning that they   [polytheistic]

included numerous gods. The ancient Hebrews were among the first of the

world's peoples to evolve a _____ religion, one centered   [monotheistic]

on belief in a single, all-powerful God. In China, Japan, and other societies

of the Far East, religions predominate that are centered not on devotion to a

god or gods but on an _____ of spirituality and human   [abstract ideal]

behavior. In addition, some social scientists have expanded the definition of

religion to include _____, or collections of beliefs and   [civil religions]

rituals that exist outside religious institutions.

A major controversy in the study of religious institutions has to do with the

role they play in social change. _____ believed that   [Karl Marx]

cultural institutions like religion are shaped by economic and political

institutions and that they function to instill in the masses the values of the

dominant class. _____, on the other hand, argued that   [Max Weber]

religion can cause major social change by instilling certain values in the members of a society, who in turn produce changes in other institutions. Religion today is a highly structured institution, with numerous _____ and _____ within a variety of [statuses; roles] _____, as well as many kinds of smaller, less [organizations] bureaucratic groups. A _____ is a religious organization [church] that has strong ties to the larger society and has at one time or another enjoyed the loyalty of most of the society's members. A _____ rejects the religious beliefs or practices of an [sect] established church and usually is formed when a group of church members splits off to form a rival organization. A third type of religious organization is the _____, which is on good terms with the religious [denomination] institution from which it developed but must compete with others for members.

A _____ is an entirely new religion. Along with sects, [cult] _____ are a major source of change in religious [cults] organizations. People who are not satisfied with established churches and denominations may form or join a _____ or [cult] _____. New religious movements arise when a [sect] _____ attracts a number of followers. This is particularly [religious innovator] likely when traditional religions fail to meet the needs of their members or when a society is undergoing rapid _____. [secularization] Membership in a religious organization is quite different from identification with a religious faith, and this is reflected in trends in religion in the United States. Among those trends are a growing tendency to practice _____ or "folk" religion and an emphasis on [unofficial] _____ as opposed to church membership. Religiosity [religiosity] refers to the depth of a person's religious feelings and how those feelings are translated into religious behavior. Studies find _____ [high] percentages of Americans believing in the existence of God and in a life after death.

In societies characterized by religious _____, one usually [pluralism] can observe the continual formation of new religious organizations.

Religious _____ are believers who are devoted to the [fundamentalists] strict observance of ritual and doctrine and lack tolerance for differences in belief and practice. In the United States fundamentalism experienced a

Harcourt Brace & Company.

resurgence during the 1980s, encouraged by _____ social   [conservative] movements.

Matching Exercise

For each of the following terms, identify the correct definition and enter the appropriate letter in the blank in front of the definition.

a. religion
b. ritual
c. sacred
d. profane
e. secularization
f. simple supernaturalism
g. animism
h. theism

i. polytheistic
j. monotheistic
k. civil religion
l. church
m. sect
n. denomination
o. cult
p. religiosity

_____1.   a new religion

_____2.   a process in which the dominance of religion over other institutions is reduced

_____3.   a term used to describe a theistic belief system that includes numerous gods.

_____4.   a formal pattern of activity that expresses symbolically a set of shared meanings.

_____5.   the depth of a person's religious feelings

_____6.   a term used to describe phenomena that are not considered sacred.

_____7.   a form of religion in which all forms of life and all aspects of the earth are inhabited by gods or supernatural powers.

_____8.   any set of coherent answers to the dilemmas of human existence that makes the world meaningful; a system of beliefs and rituals that serves to bind people together into a social group.

_____9.   a term used to describe a theistic belief system centered on belief in a single all-powerful God.

_____10.   a religious organization that reflects the beliefs and practices of existing churches; usually formed when a group leaves the church to form a rival organization.

_____11.   a collection of beliefs and rituals that exist outside religious institutions.

_____12.   a term used to describe phenomena that are regarded as extraordinary, transcendent, and outside the everyday course of events.

_____13.   a belief system that conceives of a god or gods as separate from humans and other living things on the earth.

Harcourt Brace & Company.

_____14.   a religious organization that is on good terms with the institution from which it developed but must compete with other organizations for members.

_____15.   a form of religion in which people may believe in a great force or spirit but do not have a well-defined concept of God or a set of rituals involving God.

_____16.   a religious organization that has strong ties to the larger society.

Self-Test

_____1.   Religion may be defined as
   a.   any set of coherent answers to the dilemmas of human existence.
   b.   a system of beliefs and rituals that binds people together into a social group.
   c.   a belief system that conceives of a god or gods as separate from humans and other living things.
   d.   both a and b

_____2.   The process by which the traditional dominance of religion in the cultural realm has been reduced is known as
   a.   religiosity.   c.   civil religion.
   b.   secularization.   d.   affirmative action.

_____3.   A form of religion in which all natural phenomena are part of a single force is termed
   a.   simple supernaturalism.   c.   theism.
   b.   animism.   d.   civil religion.

_____4.   In the Far East, religions tend to be based on
   a.   devotion to a god.   c.   abstract ideals.
   b.   the institutions of the state. d.   expression of deep emotions.

_____5.   A collection of beliefs, and rituals for communicating those beliefs, that exists outside of religious institutions is known as a
   a.   denomination.   c.   civil religion.
   b.   world religion.   d.   none of the above

_____6.   According to Karl Marx, the primary source of social change is
   a.   cultural institutions.   c.   technological advances.
   b.   economic institutions.   d.   secularization.

_____7.   According to Max Weber, the primary source of social change is
   a.   changes in values.   c.   population growth.
   b.   technological advances. d.   economic institutions.

_____8.   The United Methodist Church is an example of a
   a.   church.   c.   denomination.
   b.   sect.   d.   cult.

_____9.   Most major religions begin as
   a.   churches.   c.   denominations.
   b.   sects.   d.   cults.

_____10.   The majority of Americans over age fifteen identify themselves as
a.   Catholic.   c.   Jewish.
b.   Protestant.   d.   agnostic.

_____11.   Such practices as astrology, faith healing, and transcendental meditation are examples of
a.   fundamentalism.   c.   civil religion.
b.   animism.   d.   unofficial religion.

_____12.   Religiosity refers to
a.   membership in a religious organization.
b.   protection of religious pluralism.
c.   the depth of a person's religious feelings.
d.   all of the above

_____13.   Recent research on cult formation shows that
a.   cults pose a grave threat to social stability.
b.   fewer cults are formed today than in the past.
c.   cults are more successful in attracting members today than they were in the last century.
d.   people join cults because they are lonely.

_____14.   Lack of tolerance for differences in belief and practice is characteristic of
a.   animism.   c.   monotheism.
b.   fundamentalism.   d.   religiosity.

_____15.   Which of the following statements is *not* true?
a.   Religion continues to play an important role in the contemporary world.
b.   Many Americans seem to yearn for spiritual values.
c.   Recent research reveals that most Americans seek to return to traditional religious practices.
d.   Americans will continue to seek self-actualization as individuals.

T/F   16.   Until comparatively recent times, education dominated the cultural life of human societies.

T/F   17.   The major world religions identified by Weber are Christianity, Confucianism, Hinduism, Buddhism, and Islam.

T/F   18.   Sects are usually formed when a small group of church members splits off to form a rival organization.

T/F   19.   In studying the nature of religion in the United States, sociologists depend on data collected by the Census Bureau.

T/F   20.   The repeal of Prohibition represented a defeat for religious fundamentalism.

21.   Name and define the four main types of religious organization. Of the four, which two are major sources of change in religious organization?

_____

_____

_____

_____

22.   Briefly describe the distribution of religious identification in the United States. How has that distribution changed over the last two generations? How do statistics on religious identification compare with statistics on church membership and religiosity?

_____

_____

_____

_____

23.   The slogan "God is dead" was used about thirty years ago to signify the inevitability of secularization and declining religiosity. Comment on that slogan in the light of current knowledge about trends in religion.

_____

_____

_____

_____

24.   Explain Marx's phrase, "Religion is the opium of the masses."

_____

_____

_____

_____

Harcourt Brace & Company.

25.   Contrast Weber's theory of the Protestant ethic and the rise of capitalism with Marx's more materialistic view of the origins of capitalism.

_____

_____

_____

_____

CHAPTER 18 Education and Communications Media

Education for a Changing World
> The Nature of Schools
> Who Goes to School?
> Schools and Adolescent Society
> Education and Citizenship

Attainment, Achievement, and Equality
> Educational Attainment
> Barriers to Educational Attainment
> Educational Achievement
> Education and Social Mobility
> Education for Equality

The Structure of Educational Institutions
> Schools as Bureaucracies
> Changing the System: Desegregation

The Communications Media
> Media Institutions in Modern Societies
> Patterns of Media Consumption
> Television and Violence
> The Differentiation of Media Institutions
> Media Power and Its Limits

Research Frontiers: Computers, Education, and Inequality

Objectives

1. To understand how the organization and functions of schools have changed in the course of American history.
2. To be able to distinguish between educational attainment and educational achievement.
3. To be able to explain the relationship between educational institutions and social stratification.
4. To be able to define the communications media and discuss their effect on modern societies.
5. To be aware of ways in which media may or may not be subject to control by elites.

Review

To test your comprehension of the material in the chapter, cover the words in the margin with a sheet of paper and fill in the blanks in the following summary. It is not always necessary to use exactly the same words as those in the margin.

Harcourt Brace & Company.

_____ is the process by which a society transmits   [Education]
knowledge, values, norms, and ideologies and in so doing prepares young
people for adult roles and adults for new roles. It is accomplished by
specific institutions outside family, especially _____ and   [schools]
_____.   [colleges]

Schools are often cited as examples of _____   [bureaucratic]
organizations, since they tend to be characterized by a clearly defined
authority system and set of rules. A more _____   [interactionist]
viewpoint sees the school as a distinctive set of interactions and patterns of
socialization. Conflict theorists view schools as institutions whose purpose
is to maintain _____ divisions and reproduce the   [social-class]
society's existing _____ system.   [stratification]

The post–World War II _____ caused a bulge in   [baby boom]
elementary school enrollments beginning in 1952 and an expansion of the
college-age population in the 1960s. These trends were reversed in the
1960s and 1970s, but at the same time increasing numbers of
_____ have sought additional education.   [adults]

A key feature of education is the fact that schools _____   [structure]
the lives of children and adolescents. They help create a
_____ for adolescents that is separate from   [social world]
_____. Another important aspect of education in the   [adult society]
United States is the relationship between education and
_____. Education is also viewed as a tool for solving   [citizenship]
_____, especially   [social problems]
_____.   [social inequality]

Educational _____ refers to the number of years of   [attainment]
school a person has completed. It is correlated with
_____, _____,   [income; occupation]
_____, and _____.   [prestige; attitudes and
opinions]

The average American today has much more education than the average
American of the early 1940s. One effect of higher educational attainment is
"_____," in which employers require more education of   [degree inflation]
potential employees.

Educational _____ refers to how much the student   [achievement]
actually learns, measured by mastery of _____,   [reading]

Harcourt Brace & Company.

_____, and _____ skills. The steady   [writing; mathematical]

decline in mean SAT scores in the 1970s and 1980s has been viewed as a

sign that average levels of educational achievement have declined. Cross-

cultural research has shown that these deficiencies are apparent from an

early age. American parents are more likely than Asian parents to be

_____ with their children's schoolwork and to believe   [satisfied]

that the schools are doing a _____ job; they therefore are   [good]

less likely to be _____ of the schools or to demand   [critical]

_____ of their children.   [more]

Educational institutions have been criticized by observers who believe that

they hinder, rather than enhance, _____. Schools have   [social mobility]

been accused of serving as selection and certification agencies, and thereby

legitimizing _____. Higher levels of educational   [inequality]

attainment provide the _____ required for better jobs,   [credentials]

and students who are able to obtain them usually come from the

_____ and _____ classes. A factor   [middle; upper]

that has been shown to affect students' school careers is teacher

_____ regarding students, which are affected by the   [expectations]

teacher's knowledge of the student's family background.

Inequality in higher education is primarily a matter of access, that is, ability

to _____. Students from poor, working-class, and   [pay]

lower-middle-class families, as well as members of racial minority groups,

are most likely to rely on _____ colleges and   [public]

universities. Most educational researchers agree that without college

assistance for needy students, differences in educational

_____ and _____ would be much   [attainment; achievement]

greater.

The American educational system is highly _____, a fact   [bureaucratized]

that acts as a major barrier to educational change. Nevertheless, when they

have been required to change—as in the case of _____—   [desegregation]

schools have often proved to be very adaptable.

_____ are institutions that specialize in communicating   [Communications media]

information, images, and values about a society and its members. The

media are run by _____ who are skilled in producing and   [professional communi-

transmitting news and other communications. In some societies the media   cators]

Harcourt Brace & Company.

are subject to strict _____, and even in societies in which   [censorship]
the freedom of the press and other media is protected, that freedom is often
threatened by attempts to control the nature of the _____   [information]
communicated by the media.

Some sociologists have criticized the media for producing a
"_____" in which an increasing number of people have   [mass culture]
similar cultural traits and values and can be easily _____   [manipulated]
by those who control media institutions. However, data on media
consumption do not support this theory. They show that listeners and
viewers are not _____ in their tastes and are not unduly   [homogeneous]
influenced by the media. Other research has shown that there is a complex
relationship between the viewing of _____ acts on   [violent]
television and subsequent _____ behavior in some   [aggressive]
subgroups of the population.

The _____ of the communications media from other   [differentiation]
institutions is illustrated by the development of newspapers. Over time "the
press" became an independent _____ institution that is   [cultural]
also a business whose goal is to make a _____. The   [profit]
same can be said of the electronic media, the _____   [dominant]
communications media today.

Because the media in modern societies control such a large and diverse flow
of _____, they have immense power. In the United   [information]
States, they exert a powerful influence over the conduct of
_____. On the other hand, changing   [politics]
_____ have given media consumers a wider range of   [technologies]
choices, thereby limiting the power of the media to influence

_____.   [mass audiences]

Matching Exercise

For each of the following terms, identify the correct definition and enter the appropriate letter in the blank in front of the definition.

a. education
b. educational attainment
c. educational achievement

d. communications media
e. two-step flow of communication
f. opinion leader

_____1. the process in which messages communicated by the media are evaluated by certain respected individuals, who in turn influence the attitudes and behavior of others.

_____2. the number of years of school an individual has completed.

_____3. institutions that specialize in communicating information, images, and values about ourselves, our communities, and our society.

_____4. an individual who consistently influences the attitudes and behavior of others.

_____5. the process by which a society transmits knowledge, values, norms, and ideologies and in so doing prepares young people for adult roles and adults for new roles.

_____6. how much the student actually learns, measured by mastery of reading, writing, and mathematical skills.

Self-Test

_____1. From an interactionist viewpoint, the central feature of schools is
    a. their bureaucratic structure.
    b. the specific behaviors that occur there.
    c. their elaborate monitoring systems.
    d. their emphasis on credentials.

_____2. Which of the following were excluded from educational institutions in the nation's early history?
    a. children of slaves   c. girls
    b. the poor   d. all of the above

_____3. The most rapidly growing area of education is
    a. adult education.   c. elementary schools.
    b. preschool programs.   d. public universities.

_____4. The "adolescent society" or "youth culture" is a result of
    a. the growing number of dual-career families.
    b. rising expectations regarding educational attainment.
    c. television programming focusing on the generation gap.
    d. the declining role of religious organizations.

_____5. Educational attainment refers to
    a. number of years of school completed.
    b. mastery of specific subjects.
    c. employers' educational requirements.
    d. ability to read, write, and keep a family budget.

_____6. A major problem related to educational attainment is
    a. the effects of tracking.
    b. degree inflation.
    c. dropping out because of pregnancy.
    d. all of the above

_____7.   Educational achievement refers to
   a.   employers' educational requirements.
   b.   number of years of school completed.
   c.   mastery of reading, writing, and mathematical skills.
   d.   none of the above

_____8.   Which of the following statements is *not* true?
   a.   Sociologists view the school as a good example of a bureaucratic organization.
   b.   Studies have found that the experience of students in the classroom is of central importance to their later development.
   c.   Educational institutions enhance social mobility, especially for people from working-class backgrounds.
   d.   Inequality in higher education is primarily a matter of ability to pay.

_____9.   The idea that differences in jobs and social position are justified by differences in investment (hard work in school and investment in a college education) is known as
   a.   the self-fulfilling prophecy.   c.   tracking.
   b.   human-capital theory.   d.   degree inflation.

_____10.   Efforts to desegregate public schools began in
   a.   1954.   c.   the 1970s.
   b.   1964.   d.   the 1980s.

_____11.   In the United States the communications media are run by
   a.   political leaders.   c.   professional communicators.
   b.   opinion leaders.   d.   educational experts.

_____12.   Some sociologists believe that the communications media have
   a.   produced a mass culture.
   b.   caused an increase in immoral behavior.
   c.   lowered students' reading scores.
   d.   replaced oral communication.

_____13.   Studies of the relationship between televised violence and violent behavior have shown that
   a.   violence on television causes aggressive behavior by television viewers.
   b.   there is no causal connection between televised violence and violent behavior.
   c.   the effect of televised violence depends in part on the viewer's emotional condition.
   d.   none of the above

_____14.   The growth of newspapers was closely linked to the growth of
   a.   corporations.   c.   information technologies.
   b.   political parties.   d.   cities.

_____15.   Which of the following statements is *not* true?
   a.   Total control over the media is a major goal of oppressive regimes.
   b.   The media exert a powerful influence over the conduct of American politics.
   c.   Changes in media technologies are making it more difficult for powerful individuals to manipulate mass audiences.
   d.   Researchers have found a direct link between persuasive messages and actual behavior.

T/F   16.   By 1980 all the nations of the world had mass educational systems.

T/F   17.   The post–World War II baby boom caused a massive expansion of the college-age population in the 1950s.

T/F   18.   The primary reason for dropping out of school is poor academic performance.

T/F   19.   In the United States the messages communicated by the media are mainly political, religious, or educational.

T/F   20.   In his study of the selection of items to be reported as news, Herbert Gans found that such decisions are heavily influenced by the desires of advertisers.

21.   Distinguish between educational attainment and educational achievement and indicate the social problems associated with each.

_____

_____

_____

_____

22.   The O. J. Simpson trial was perhaps the most widely viewed trial in history. Do you think that media access to the proceedings made a contribution to the public's understanding of the American criminal justice system? Did media exposure make it difficult for the parties involved to obtain a fair hearing of their case? How would you decide on the issue of television access in future celebrity trials?

_____

_____

_____

_____

23.   Do schools help reproduce patterns of inequality and class stratification, or do they contribute to social mobility? Defend your answer with examples from the text.

_____

_____

_____

_____

24.   How do class conflict and social movements help bring about change in educational institutions?

_____

_____

_____

_____

25.   Sociological evidence does not lend much support to the thesis that media owners control how news is communicated. Explain why this may be the case.

_____

_____

_____

_____

Harcourt Brace & Company.

CHAPTER 19   Economic Institutions

Sociology and Economics
Markets and the Division of Labor
    The Nature of Markets
    Markets and the World Economic System
Economics and the State
    Political–Economic Ideologies
    Political Economics in Practice: After the Cold War
Workers, Managers, and Corporations
    Worker Alienation
    Individuals and Corporations
    Sociological Perspectives on the Workplace
Research Frontiers: Global Change and Adapting Economies

Objectives

1. To understand that economic institutions are those that are concerned with organizing the production and distribution of goods and services.
2. To be able to distinguish between economic and sociological approaches to economic institutions.
3. To appreciate the role of markets as the economic institution that regulates exchange behavior.
4. To become aware of the implications of the spread of markets into societies throughout the world.
5. To be able to describe the major economic ideologies that have shaped world history, from mercantilism to welfare capitalism.
6. To understand sociology's contribution to the theory and practice of industrial management.
7. To be able to apply the interactionist perspective to the study of professions.

Review

To test your comprehension of the material in the chapter, cover the words in the margin with a sheet of paper and fill in the blanks in the following summary. It is not always necessary to use exactly the same words as those in the margin.

Economics is the study of how individuals and societies choose to employ

_____ resources to produce various commodities and   [scarce]

_____ them among groups in the society. Sociologists   [distribute]

are also concerned with how individuals and societies make such choices,

but much of their research focuses on how _____ affect   [cultural norms] those choices. The main subjects of sociological research in this area are

_____ and the division of labor, the interactions between   [markets]

_____ and economic institutions, and the nature of   [government]

_____ and _____ .   [jobs; professions]

A hallmark of an industrial society is the production of commodities and

services to be exchanged in _____ . A   [markets]

_____ is an economic institution that regulates exchange   [market]

behavior. In a market, different _____ are established for   [values]

particular goods and services; these are usually expressed in terms of a

common measure of exchange, or _____ . Market   [currency]

transactions are governed by agreements, or _____ , in   [contracts]

which a seller agrees to supply a particular item and a buyer agrees to pay

for it. The spread of markets throughout the world began in the late

_____ century as a result of the development of new   [fifteenth]

technologies that facilitated _____ . Today world markets   [trade]

are dominated by _____ , economic enterprises that have   [multinational corpor-

headquarters in one country and conduct business in one or more other   ations]

countries.

The fate of societies throughout the world has been strongly influenced by

economic ideologies. _____ held that the wealth of a   [Mercantilism]

nation could be measured by its holdings of gold, so the best economic

system was one that increased the nation's _____ .   [exports]

_____ , on the other hand, argued that a society's wealth   [Laissez-faire capitalism]

could be measured only by its capacity to produce goods and services—that

is, its resources of _____ , _____ ,   [land; labor]

and _____ . The major institutions of capitalism are   [machinery]

_____ and   [private property]

_____ .   [free markets]

_____ arose out of the belief that private property and   [Socialism]

personal profit should be replaced by public ownership of property and

sharing of profits. According to Marx, the _____ state   [socialist]

would be controlled by the workers, who would determine what should be

produced and how it should be distributed. Soviet-style socialist societies

were characterized until recently by _____ economies, in   [command]

which the state commands economic institutions to supply a specific amount

Harcourt Brace & Company.

of each product and to sell it at a particular price. _____   [Democratic socialism]
holds that private property must continue to exist but that large corporations
should be owned by the nation or, if they are in private hands, required to
be run for the benefit of all citizens.

In _____, markets determine what goods and services   [welfare capitalism]
will be produced and how, but the government regulates economic
competition. In addition, the state invests in the society's

_____ through policies promoting education, health care,   [human resources]
and social welfare.

The end of the cold war has raised the question of how the transition from
command economies to _____   [entrepreneurial-style]

_____ economies will be carried out in the former   [market]
socialist nations. Those nations are groping toward

_____ economic systems, but in the meantime they retain   [social-democratic]
elements of the older command system and the unregulated

_____. In the United States, the transition from an   [black market]
economy based on the production of _____ to one based   [goods]
on the provision of _____ has resulted in the   [services]
displacement of thousands of skilled workers into lower-paid jobs in the

_____ sector. These trends appear to signal a change in   [service]
the basic "_____" in which individuals who work hard   [social contract]
can expect increases in their living standards.

American workers feel an organizational and cultural gap separating them
from _____ even when they share the same goals. Many   [managers]
sociologists use the concept of _____ _____ to explain this gap.   [alienation]
This term refers to the feeling of being powerless to control one's own
destiny. At work, people may feel _____ because their   [alienated]
labor is divided up into activities that are meaningless to them.

In the United States and other industrialized societies, the

_____ has gained ever-greater dominance over other   [corporation]
economic institutions. Corporations are "_____" that can   [fictional persons]
incur debts and liabilities on their own account. In this century the
importance of corporations has come to outweigh that of

_____ in most of the institutional sectors of society, and   [individuals]
the individual is often at a disadvantage in dealings with corporations.

Harcourt Brace & Company.

The _____ approach to labor–management relations   [scientific management]
attempted to increase productivity by determining how each job could be
performed most _____ and by using   [efficiently]
_____ payment systems to induce workers to produce   [piecework]
more. Efforts to determine what conditions would result in the highest rates
of worker productivity led to the recognition that
_____ is   [cooperation between
an important ingredient in worker satisfaction and output. This gave rise to   workers and managers]
the _____ approach to management, which seeks to   [human relations]
improve cooperation between workers and managers.
_____ believe that the human relations approach fails to   [Conflict theorists]
consider the basic causes of worker–management conflict. They study how
_____ and _____ both at work and   [social class; status]
outside the workplace influence relations between workers and managers.
Interactionist theorists have devoted considerable study to
_____, or the way in which occupations attempt to gain   [professionalization]
the status of professions, and to the processes of _____   [professional social-
(i.e., learning the formal and informal norms of the profession).   ization]

Matching Exercise

For each of the following terms, identify the correct definition and enter the appropriate letter in the
blank in front of the definition.

a. market
b. technology
c. multinational corporation
d. mercantilism
e. laissez-faire capitalism
f. socialism
g. democratic socialism
h. welfare capitalism
i. alienation
j. profession

_____1.   an economic philosophy based on the belief that the wealth of a nation can be
              measured by its capacity to produce goods and services (i.e., its resources of land,
              labor, and machinery) and that these can be maximized by free trade.

_____2.   tools, procedures, and forms of social organization that increase human productive
              capacity.

_____3. the feeling of being powerless to control one's own destiny; a worker's feeling of powerlessness owing to inability to control the work process.

_____4. an economic philosophy based on the belief that private property may exist at the same time that large corporations are owned by the state and run for the benefit of all citizens.

_____5. an occupation with a body of knowledge and a developed intellectual technique that are transmitted by a formal educational process and testing procedures.

_____6. an economic enterprise that has headquarters in one country and conducts business activities in one or more other countries.

_____7. an economic philosophy based on the concept of public ownership of property and sharing of profits, together with the belief that economic decisions should be controlled by the workers.

_____8. an economic institution that regulates exchange behavior through the establishment of different values for particular goods and services.

_____9. an economic philosophy in which markets determine what goods will be produced and how, but the government regulates economic competition.

_____10. an economic philosophy based on the belief that the wealth of a nation can be measured by its holdings of gold or other precious metals and that the state should control trade.

Self-Test

_____1. Sociologists who study economic institutions are interested in how economic choices are affected by
    a. production technologies.   c. historical events.
    b. cultural norms.   d. currency values.

_____2. Economic institutions that regulate exchange behavior are
    a. markets.   c. contracts.
    b. corporations.   d. professions.

_____3. In the modern world, economic resources are increasingly controlled by
    a. great empires.   c. multinational corporations.
    b. colonial powers.   d. government agencies.

_____4. The economic philosophy known as mercantilism held that a nation's wealth could be measured by
    a. its capacity to produce goods and services.
    b. its holdings of gold and other precious metals.
    c. the average income of its working class.
    d. the average educational level of its citizens.

_____5. The best-known proponent of laissez-faire capitalism was
    a. Adam Smith.   c. John Maynard Keynes.
    b. Karl Marx.   d. Paul Samuelson.

_____6.   Which of the following is characteristic of the economic and political philosophy known as socialism?
a.   elimination of markets
b.   state-controlled economic planning
c.   worker control over industrial decisions
d.   all of the above

_____7.   An economic philosophy that holds that large corporations should be owned by the nation but economic decisions should be made democratically is known as
a.   laissez-faire capitalism.   c.   democratic socialism.
b.   welfare capitalism.   d.   communism.

_____8.   Which of the following economic philosophies asserts that the state should invest in the society's human resources?
a.   mercantilism   c.   welfare capitalism
b.   laissez-faire capitalism   d.   none of the above

_____9.   Which of the following did *not* occur in the former socialist nations?
a.   State planning agencies were stripped of their power.
b.   The black market was eliminated.
c.   The right to own property was established through legislation.
d.   Noncompetitive factories were closed.

_____10.   Which of the following is viewed as a sign of decline in the U.S. economy?
a.   The number of dual-earner households has increased dramatically since the 1950s.
b.   The wages of less educated workers have declined significantly.
c.   There is a growing disparity between the incomes of professionals and those of people with jobs requiring less formal education.
d.   all of the above

_____11.   One of the distinctive features of Japanese factories is that
a.   many workers have permanent tenure.
b.   workers and managers are viewed as natural adversaries.
c.   workers consider their work to be an intrusion into their social life.
d.   all of the above

_____12.   The gap between workers and managers is often explained in terms of the concept of
a.   anomie.   c.   exploitation.
b.   the Hawthorne effect.   d.   alienation.

_____13.   The scientific management approach to labor–management relations was developed by
a.   Frederick W. Taylor.   c.   William F. Whyte.
b.   Elton Mayo.   d.   Michael Burawoy.

_____14.   Efforts to improve cooperation between workers and managers in order to achieve the organization's goals are characteristic of
a.   scientific management.
b.   the human relations approach.
c.   conflict-oriented industrial sociology.
d.   professionalization.

_____15. Sociologists who study professions are interested in
a.   the way occupations attempt to gain the status of professions.
b.   role relationships within professions.
c.   the processes of professional socialization.
d.   all of the above

T/F   16. Preindustrial societies are characterized by the production of commodities and services to be exchanged in markets.

T/F   17. For the past two centuries the exploitation of the resources of colonial territories has been directed by multinational corporations.

T/F   18. The laissez-faire economists believed that private property and personal profits should be eliminated.

T/F   19. Sociologists generally agree that the transformation of the United States from an industrial to a postindustrial society is inevitable.

T/F   20. Japanese firms tend to avoid worker alienation by strengthening the role of the small group.

21. Sociologists often apply an economic approach to the study of situations that are not related to the production of goods and services, such as the choice of a mate or the decision to have a child. Can you think of an example from your own experience in which you have made a choice of this nature by calculating the "price" in terms of opportunities gained or lost?

_____

_____

_____

_____

22. The text describes several economic philosophies, each of which has received considerable support in different historical periods and different regions of the world. Compare those philosophies, and identify the one that is characteristic of the United States today.

_____

_____

_____

_____

Harcourt Brace & Company.

23.   Do you agree with Daniel Bell that the United States is becoming a postindustrial society? If so, do you view this transition as a crisis? How has it affected people with whom you are acquainted?

_____

_____

_____

_____

24.   Define a profession and show how some occupations seek professional status.

_____

_____

_____

_____

25.   Compare Japanese and American corporations in terms of organizational norms and employee–management relations.

_____

_____

_____

_____

CHAPTER 20   Politics and Political Institutions

The Nature of Politics and Political Institutions
Politics, Power, and Authority
Legitimacy and Authority
The Political Ecology of States and Territories
States and Borders
Citizenship and Political Participation
Political Institutions in Modern Societies
Democratic Political Systems
Perspectives on Political Institutions
Structural Prerequisites of Democracy and the Rule of Law
The Power Elite Model
The Pluralist Model
Politics and Social Interaction
Military Institutions
The Economic Role of the Military
Military Socialization
Social Change and Military Institutions
Research Frontiers: Trends in Political Participation

Objectives

1. To understand that politics is a set of processes whereby members of a society compete for the power to control the behavior of others.
2. To be able to define the concept of legitimacy and show how it is realized in the political culture of a society.
3. To appreciate the place of political institutions in nation-states.
4. To understand citizenship as the status of membership in a nation-state and to recognize the implications of noncitizenship.
5. To be able to define and give examples of different types of political organizations.
6. To be able to distinguish among major types of political regimes and their distinctive institutions.
7. To be able to describe the obstacles and threats to democratic political institutions that may be found in social conditions as well as in human nature.

Review

To test your comprehension of the material in the chapter, cover the words in the margin with a sheet of paper and fill in the blanks in the following summary. It is not always necessary to use exactly the same words as those in the margin.

Harcourt Brace & Company.

Politics determines "who gets what, when, and how." The basis of politics is competition for _____, or the ability to control the behavior of others, even against their will. _____ is institutionalized power, or power whose exercise is governed by the norms and statuses of organizations. Sets of norms and statuses that specialize in the exercise of power and authority are _____, and the set of political institutions that operate in a particular society forms the _____.

Although a state can exercise its power through the use of _____, eventually this will not be enough to govern a society. When people consent to be governed without the use of force, the state is said to be _____. _____ is a society's ability to engender and maintain the belief that the existing political institutions are the most appropriate for that society. It is the basis of a society's _____—the cultural norms, values, and symbols that support and justify its political institutions.

According to Max Weber, the political cultures of different societies give rise to three different types of authority: _____, _____, and _____. Perhaps the strongest and most dangerous political force in the world today is _____, the belief of a people that they have the right and the duty to constitute themselves as a nation-state.

The most important political territory in world affairs is the _____, the largest territory within which a society's political institutions can operate without having to face challenges to their sovereignty. The borders that mark off one nation-state from others do not always correspond to what people believe to be the rightful boundaries of their _____.

_____ is the status of membership in a nation-state. The rights of citizenship include _____ (e.g., freedom of speech, thought, and faith), _____ (e.g., the right to vote), and _____ (e.g., the right to a certain level of economic welfare and security). The question of who is entitled to full _____ in politics is a key issue at the local level as well as at the national level.

[power]
[Authority]
[political institutions]
[state]
[force]
[legitimate; Legitimacy]
[political culture]
[traditional]
[charismatic; legal]
[nationalism]
[nation-state]
[societies]
[Citizenship]
[civil rights]
[political rights]
[social rights]
[participation]

Harcourt Brace & Company.

Modern nations are governed by _____ and   [elected]

_____ officials whose authority is defined by   [appointed]

_____. In order to prevent abuses of authority, modern   [laws]

political institutions usually specify some form of _____   [separation of

in which abuses by one institution can be remedied by others.   powers]

_____ are organizations of people who join together in   [Political parties]

order to gain legitimate control of state authority. Parties that accept the rule

of other legitimate parties form a "_____" that monitors   [loyal opposition]

the actions of the ruling party and prevents the emergence of

_____, or rule by a few people who stay in office   [oligarchy]

indefinitely. Regimes that accept no limits to their power and seek to exert

their rule at all levels of society are known as _____   [totalitarian]

regimes.

_____ means rule by the nation's citizens: Citizens have   [Democracy]

the right to participate in public decision making, and those who govern do

so with the _____ of the governed. In the British   [explicit consent]

_____ system, elections are held in which the party that   [parliamentary]

wins a majority of the seats in the legislature "forms a government": The

leader of the party becomes the head of government and appoints other party

members to major offices. In the American _____   [representative]

system, the party whose candidate is elected president need not have a

majority of the seats in the legislature. In nations or regions in which a

single party is dominant, _____ political systems are   [oligarchical]

more likely to develop.

Functionalist theorists assert that certain _____ must   [structural prerequisites]

exist in a society for democratic political institutions to develop and operate.

Among these are high levels of _____,   [economic development]

_____, and _____, as well as a   [urbanization; literacy]

culture that tolerates dissent. The _____ model holds that   [power elite]

the presence of democratic institutions does not mean that a society is

democratic; political decisions are actually controlled by an

_____ of rich and powerful individuals. This view is   [elite]

challenged by the _____ model, which holds that   [pluralist]

political decisions are influenced by a variety of _____   [interest groups]

through a process of coalition building and bargaining.

Harcourt Brace & Company.

Many political thinkers have been concerned with the relationship between social interaction and political institutions. Among the most influential was _____, who argued that political institutions must be [Machiavelli] based on the recognition that human beings are capable of evil as well as good. This recognition played a major part in the planning of the government of the _____, in which each branch of the [United States] government is able to check _____ by the other [abuses of power] branches.

In modern nation-states _____ is a major concern [political communi-cation] for those out of power as well as those in power. It is important to analyze political communications and to "read between the lines" of political rhetoric. This is particularly true in societies characterized by _____ and [mass publics] _____ communication techniques. [sophisticated]

A major question in political sociology is how states can control their _____ institutions. A society cannot remain [military] _____ very long if the military usurps the authority [democratic] granted to it by _____ institutions. One factor that [civilian] contributes to this problem is the fact that the military is staffed by _____ soldiers for whom service in the armed forces is a [professional] _____. Another factor is the immense influence of the [career] military on the _____. On the other hand, [economy] _____ instills norms and values that may contribute to [military socialization] social control of the military.

Matching Exercise

For each of the following terms, identify the correct definition and enter the appropriate letter in the blank in front of the definition.

a. power
b. authority
c. political institution
d. state
e. legitimacy
f. traditional authority
g. charismatic authority
h. legal authority
i. nationalism

j. nation-state
k. citizenship
l. demagogue
m. political party
n. oligarchy
o. totalitarian regime
p. democracy
q. patronage
r. power elite model

s. pluralist model
t. interest group
u. lobbying

_____1.   the largest territory within which a society's political institutions can operate without having to face challenges to their sovereignty.

_____2.   a leader who uses personal charisma and political symbols to manipulate public opinion.

_____3.   jobs and economic benefits that party leaders can exchange for votes and political influence.

_____4.   power whose exercise is governed by the norms and statuses of organizations.

_____5.   rule by a few people who stay in office indefinitely rather than for limited terms.

_____6.   a theory stating that no single group controls political decisions; instead, a plurality of interest groups influence those decisions through a process of coalition building and bargaining.

_____7.   the ability of a society to engender and maintain the belief that the existing political institutions are the most appropriate for that society.

_____8.   a set of norms and statuses pertaining to the exercise of power and authority.

_____9.   an organization that attempts to influence elected and appointed officials regarding a specific issue or set of issues.

_____10.   authority that comes to an individual through a personal calling, often claimed to be inspired by supernatural powers, and is legitimated by people's belief that the leader does indeed have God-given powers.

_____11.   the belief of a people that they have the right and the duty to constitute themselves as a nation-state.

_____12.   the status of membership in a nation-state

_____13.   a regime that accepts no limits to its power and seeks to exert its rule at all levels of society.

_____14.   a political system in which all citizens have the right to participate in public decision making.

_____15.   the ability to control the behavior of others, even against their will.

_____16.   the process whereby interest groups seek to persuade legislators to vote in their favor on particular bills.

_____17.   authority that is legitimated by people's belief in the supremacy of the law; obedience is owed not to a person but to a set of impersonal principles.

_____18.   authority that is hereditary and is legitimated by traditional values, particularly people's idea of the sacred.

Harcourt Brace & Company.

_____19.   an organization of people who join together to gain legitimate control of state authority.

_____20.   the set of political institutions operating in a particular society.

_____21.   a theory stating that political decisions are controlled by an elite group of rich and powerful individuals even in societies with democratic political institutions.

Self-Test

_____1.   The ability to control the behavior of others, even against their will, is
    a.   authority.   c.   politics.
    b.   legitimacy.   d.   power.

_____2.   In the long run, a society cannot be governed without
    a.   the use of force or coercion.
    b.   the consent of the governed.
    c.   a democratic political system.
    d.   all of the above

_____3.   The norms, values, and symbols that support a society's political institutions are referred to as its
    a.   civil religion.   c.   political ecology.
    b.   political culture.   d.   rights of citizenship.

_____4.   The longest peaceful and uncontested national boundary in the world is the border between
    a.   the United States and Canada.   c.   China and Russia.
    b.   France and Germany.   d.   Norway and Sweden.

_____5.   Which of the following is *not* considered a right of citizenship?
    a.   freedom of speech
    b.   the right to vote
    c.   the right to a certain level of economic welfare
    d.   the right to hold public office

_____6.   According to Edward Shils, which of the following is an essential institution of a modern state?
    a.   a rational administration
    b.   a party system
    c.   institutions for maintaining order
    d.   all of the above

_____7.   A leader who uses personal charisma and political symbols to manipulate public opinion is
    a.   an oligarch.   c.   a junta.
    b.   a demagogue.   d.   a party boss.

_____8.   An organization of people who join together in order to gain legitimate control of state authority is
    a.   an oligarchy.   c.   a political party.
    b.   an interest group.   d.   none of the above

_____9.   A coup d'état usually results in the establishment of
a.   an oligarchy.   c.   a loyal opposition.
b.   a democracy.   d.   a parliamentary system.

_____10.   A political system in which the party that wins a majority of the seats in the legislature "forms a government" is a
a.   totalitarian system.   c.   representative system.
b.   junta system.   d.   parliamentary system.

_____11.   According to Seymour Martin Lipset, which of the following is a structural prerequisite of democracy?
a.   a high degree of urbanization   c.   a culture that values equality
b.   a high rate of literacy   d.   all of the above

_____12.   The chief proponent of the "power elite" model is
a.   Niccolò Machiavelli.   c.   Dwight D. Eisenhower.
b.   C. Wright Mills.   d.   Aristotle.

_____13.   The National Rifle Association is an example of
a.   a junta.   c.   an interest group.
b.   an industrial–military complex.   d.   a political party.

_____14.   Machiavelli believed that political institutions had to be based on the recognition that
a.   human beings are capable of evil.
b.   creating political institutions is a slow process.
c.   the military has undue influence over other institutions.
d.   the mass media are essential to political power.

_____15.   Tocqueville believed that
a.   democratic societies would provide fertile soil for the rise of demagogues.
b.   the United States could be torn by political conflict.
c.   Americans' belief in the legitimacy of their political institutions would carry them through any crisis that might arise.
d.   all of the above

T/F 16.   The basis of politics is competition for power.

T/F 17.   The borders of nation-states usually correspond to the boundaries of societies.

T/F 18.   Modern political institutions usually specify some form of separation of powers.

T/F 19.   An oligarchy is an organization of people who join together to gain legitimate control of state authority.

T/F 20.   It is possible for a one-party state or region to be democratic.

21.   Identify some of the norms, values, and symbols that constitute the political culture of the United States.

_____

_____

_____

22.   The proposed Equal Rights Amendment to the U.S. Constitution, which was not ratified by the required number of states, reads as follows: "Equality of rights under the law shall not be denied or abridged by the United States or by any State on account of sex." In the absence of this constitutional amendment, do you think women in the United States have the full rights of citizenship? Why or why not?

_____

_____

_____

_____

23.   Describe what is meant by the political ecology of nations. What place do political boundaries and military institutions have in establishing this political ecology?

_____

_____

_____

_____

24.   Under what conditions do states experience crises of legitimacy? What changes must occur if the resolution of a crisis is to be considered democratic? Under what conditions would a solution be considered authoritarian?

_____

_____

_____

_____

25.   According to Lipset's theory, what are the sociological prerequisites for democratic political institutions?

_____

_____

_____

_____

Harcourt Brace & Company.

CHAPTER 21   Science, Technology, and Medicine

The Nature of Science and Technology
Scientific Institutions: The Sociological View
    The Sociology of Science
    The Norms of Science
Technology in Modern Societies
    Dimensions of Technology
    Technological Dualism
    Technology and Social Change
    The Quest for Energy
    Technology in Everyday Life
Medical Technology
    The Hospital: From Poorhouse to Healing Institution
    Hypertrophy in Health Care?
    Medical Sociology
The Impact of Technology
    Technological Systems
    Environmental Stress
**Research Frontiers: Environmental Change and
Violent Conflict**

Objectives

1. To be able to define science and technology.
2. To understand the interactionist and institutional approaches to the study of scientific institutions.
3. To appreciate the organizational dimension of technology.
4. To become aware of technological dualism.
5. To be able to describe the evolution of medicine.
6. To appreciate the need for technology assessment, especially the assessment of total systems and environmental impact.

Review

To test your comprehension of the material in the chapter, cover the words in the margin with a sheet of paper and fill in the blanks in the following summary. It is not always necessary to use exactly the same words as those in the margin.

Harcourt Brace & Company.

A hallmark of the modern social order is the conduct of
_____ research in universities and other research   [scientific]
organizations. _____ is knowledge obtained as a result   [Science]
of the process of developing and testing hypotheses.

_____ science is scientific investigation devoted to the   [Pure]
pursuit of knowledge for its own sake. _____ science is   [Applied]
the application of known scientific principles to a practical problem.

_____ involves the use of tools and knowledge to   [Technology]
manipulate the physical environment to achieve desired practical goals.
Technology is much _____ than science, but the   [older]
discoveries of modern science are creating new _____ at   [technologies]
a rapid rate and have greatly expanded the human capacity to live in and
exploit different _____. Negative effects of technological [habitats]
change have led to calls for _____, or development that   [sustainable development]
does not damage the environment or create new environmental burdens.

The _____ approach to the study of scientific institutions [interactionist]
focuses on the scientific community or communities, the network of
_____ and _____   [communication; social
among scientists. A well-known study based on this perspective found that   relationships]
in many cases scientific researchers do not test and refute existing theories,
but assume that they are valid and use them as a _____   [paradigm]
for future research. This view of the scientific community implies that
science is _____ from the rest of society and that the   [insulated]
problems scientists choose to solve are determined by the tradition of
research in their field.

The _____ approach to the study of science asks why   [institutional]
science develops differently in different societies. In this view, certain
conditions encourage the development of scientific institutions. They
include recognition of _____ as a legitimate way of   [empirical research]
acquiring new knowledge. In addition, science must be
_____ from other fields. However, scientific institutions   [independent]
are never entirely separate from other institutions because scientific research
is often supported by _____ or   [government]
_____, a situation that puts pressure on scientists to meet [industry]
the _____ needs of those institutions.   [practical]

One of the most basic norms of scientific institutions is

_____: The truth of scientific knowledge must be   [universalism]

determined by the impersonal criteria of the scientific method. Another norm

of science is the _____ ownership of scientific findings,   [common]

although such findings sometimes bear the name of the person who first

published them. A third norm of scientific institutions is

_____, meaning that scientists do not allow the desire   [disinterestedness]

for personal gain to influence the reporting and evaluation of results.

The technologies produced by scientific research are a major force in

shaping and changing other _____. The basic   [institutions]

dimensions of technology are physical devices or _____,   [apparatus]

the _____ associated with their use, and the   [activities]

organizational _____ within which those activities are   [networks]

carried out. The phrase "_____" is sometimes used to   [technological dualism]

refer to the fact that technological changes often have both positive and

negative effects.

Sociologists recognize that social _____ are often slow   [institutions]

to adapt to changing technologies. This recognition forms the basis of the

theory known as _____. The time required for social   [cultural lag]

institutions to adapt to technological change can be reduced by the process

of _____, or efforts to anticipate the consequences of   [technology assessment]

particular technologies for individuals and for society as a whole.

The complex interactions between technology and other aspects of the social

order are illustrated by the case of medical technology. Until relatively

recently, physicians were powerless either to check the progress of disease

or to prolong life. _____ research led to the discovery of   [Scientific]

the causes of many diseases during the nineteenth century, but in the

twentieth century a vast array of _____ have been   [technologies]

developed both for the prevention and cure of illnesses and for the long-

term care of terminally ill patients.

The technologies used in the diagnosis and treatment of serious illnesses

require extremely _____ equipment and highly   [expensive]

_____ personnel. This has caused health care to become   [trained]

very expensive, and as a result some groups in the population are unable to

obtain adequate care. Some critics claim that extreme emphasis on

Harcourt Brace & Company.

_____ progress has created a situation in which the   [technological]

needs of the patient are subordinated to those of the providers of health care.

In recent years _____ have been faced with the challenge   [medical sociologists]

of helping society cope with the ethical issues that arise as it becomes

increasingly possible to prolong human life by _____   [artificial]

means.

The increasing complexity of modern technology had led to a new kind of

catastrophe: the failure of whole _____. The enormous   [systems]

risks associated with complex technologies have led many observers to call

for a more thorough _____ of the potential impact of   [assessment]

new technologies before they are put into operation. This is especially

important from the standpoint of protection of the _____.   [environment]

Matching Exercise

For each of the following terms, identify the correct definition and enter the appropriate letter in the blank in front of the definition.

a. science
b. technology
c. sustainable development
d. paradigm
e. cultural lag
f. technology assessment

_____1.   the time required for social institutions to adapt to a major technological change.

_____2.   the use of tools and knowledge to manipulate the physical environment in order to achieve desired practical goals.

_____3.   efforts to anticipate the consequences of particular technologies for individuals and for society as a whole.

_____4.   knowledge obtained as a result of the process of developing and testing hypotheses.

_____5.   a general way of seeing the world that dictates what kind of scientific work should be done and what kinds of theory are acceptable.

_____6.   development that does not damage the environment or create new environmental burdens.

Self-Test

_____1.   Basically, science is
     a.   research.   c.   solving problems.
     b.   knowledge.   d.   using tools.

_____2.   Pure science is
     a.   the use of tools and knowledge to manipulate the physical environment.
     b.   the application of known scientific principles to a practical problem.
     c.   scientific investigation devoted to the pursuit of knowledge for its own sake.
     d.   efforts to anticipate the consequences of particular technologies.

_____3.   According to Thomas Kuhn, scientists
     a.   spend their time testing hypotheses.
     b.   are dedicated to refuting existing theories.
     c.   use new research methods whenever possible.
     d.   assume that current theories are valid.

_____4.   The norm that states that the truth of scientific knowledge must be determined by the criteria of the scientific method is
     a.   universalism.   c.   disinterestedness.
     b.   publication.   d.   none of the above

_____5.   The norm that states that a scientist does not allow the desire for personal gain to influence the reporting of results is
     a.   universalism.   c.   publication.
     b.   common ownership.   d.   disinterestedness.

_____6.   Which of the following is *not* a basic dimension of technology?
     a.   tool, machines, and gadgets   c.   the scientific method
     b.   procedures and routines   d.   organizational networks

_____7.   The increased unemployment that sometimes accompanies automation is an example of
     a.   cultural lag.   c.   hypertrophy.
     b.   technological dualism.   d.   a paradigm.

_____8.   The delay between the advent of cable television and the development of material for the new channels is an example of
     a.   cultural lag.   c.   technological dualism.
     b.   technology assessment.   d.   a "long boom."

_____9.   Throughout history a central aspect of technological change has been the quest for new
     a.   means of population control.   c.   sources of energy.
     b.   forms of warfare.   d.   types of machinery.

_____10.   Which of the following statements is *not* true?
    a.   Research on the impact of new technologies has not kept pace with technological innovation.
    b.   Sociologists can assume that the effects of innovations are experienced by everyone in more or less the same way.
    c.   The uses of technologies may not conform with what their innovators intended.
    d.   Many sociologists believe that technologies should be thought of as facilitators of human action.

_____11.   Which of the following statements is true?
    a.   Medicine became differentiated from religion in the nineteenth century.
    b.   The discovery of the causes of many diseases led physicians to intervene more actively in curing their patients.
    c.   Rates of infant mortality decreased dramatically as a result of the sophisticated techniques of modern medicine.
    d.   none of the above

_____12.   The first hospitals were
    a.   institutions for medical care and research.
    b.   public facilities for the care of invalids and the mentally ill.
    c.   community centers for the care of the sick and the poor.
    d.   asylums for orphans and the aged.

_____13.   Some critics claim that the American health-care system is suffering from
    a.   cultural lag.   c.   disinterestedness.
    b.   technological lag.   d.   hypertrophy.

_____14.   According to Paul Starr, the problems of the American health-care system stem from
    a.   physicians' development of narrow specialties.
    b.   hospitals' investment in specialized equipment.
    c.   the emergence of medical insurance.
    d.   all of the above

_____15.   According to Charles Perrow, the major cause of technological catastrophes in the modern world is
    a.   malfunctioning apparatus.
    b.   ineffective safety precautions.
    c.   failures of whole systems.
    d.   overworked maintenance personnel.

T/F   16.   Technology is much older than science.

T/F   17.   Unlike European nations, the United States has created a single set of policies for the support of science.

T/F   18.   Organizational networks are a significant dimension of technology.

T/F   19.   The cultural lag theory fails to account for the effects of social power.

T/F   20.   Present energy policies favor what Amory Lovins terms "soft" energy paths.

21.   Distinguish between science and technology and describe how they influence each other.

_____

_____

_____

_____

22.   What are some of the basic norms of science? Can you think of cases in which each of those norms has been violated?

_____

_____

_____

_____

23.   What are three basic dimensions of technology? Describe a specific technological system in terms of those dimensions.

_____

_____

_____

_____

24.   Sociologists emphasize the organizational dimension of technology as essential to understanding the influence of technology on social change. Explain and offer some specific examples.

_____

_____

_____

25.   Explain what is meant by hypertrophy in health care and how it has arisen. What steps are being considered to address the problem?

_____

_____

_____

CHAPTER 1   Answer Key

Answers to Matching Exercise

1. d
2. h
3. k
4. e
5. j
6. f

7. b
8. i
9. g
10. c
11. a

Answers to Self-Test

1. d
2. a
3. b
4. b
5. c
6. d
7. c
8. a
9. d
10. a

11. c
12. b
13. a
14. d
15. d
16. T
17. T
18. F
19. F
20. T

CHAPTER 2   Answer Key

Answers to Matching Exercise

1. d
2. j
3. n
4. l
5. a
6. f
7. k
8. e
9. i
10. b
11. o
12. m

13. q
14. w
15. c
16. s
17. g
18. r
19. v
20. h
21. t
22. p
23. u

Answers to Self-Test

1. c
2. b
3. b
4. d
5. a
6. c
7. d
8. b
9. a
10. b

11. c
12. d
13. a
14. c
15. d
16. T
17. F
18. T
19. T
20. F

CHAPTER 3　Answer Key

Answers to Matching Exercise

1. o	14. c
2. s	15. y
3. b	16. p
4. q	17. z
5. l	18. m
6. n	19. t
7. x	20. i
8. h	21. v
9. r	22. d
10. j	23. w
11. a	24. k
12. g	25. e
13. u	26. f

Answers to Self-Test

1. d	11. b
2. a	12. d
3. d	13. b
4. c	14. d
5. b	15. c
6. b	16. F
7. c	17. T
8. a	18. F
9. a	19. T
10. c	20. F

CHAPTER 4　Answer Key

Answers to Matching Exercise

1. o	14. e
2. f	15. y
3. k	16. l
4. u	17. s
5. c	18. x
6. q	19. d
7. m	20. v
8. t	21. w
9. a	22. j
10. p	23. n
11. r	24. i
12. g	25. h
13. b	

Harcourt Brace & Company.

Answers to Self-Test

1. b	11. a
2. d	12. b
3. c	13. d
4. a	14. c
5. c	15. a
6. a	16. F
7. b	17. T
8. d	18. T
9. b	19. F
10. c	20. F

CHAPTER 5   Answer Key

Answers to Matching Exercise

1. g	10. j
2. r	11. q
3. d	12. f
4. e	13. k
5. j	14. c
6. a	15. o
7. b	16. h
8. n	17. l
9. m	18. p

Answers to Self-Test

1. b	11. b
2. c	12. b
3. c	13. a
4. d	14. c
5. c	15. b
6. d	16. F
7. a	17. F
8. d	18. T
9. d	19. T
10. d	20. F

CHAPTER 6   Answer Key

Answers to Matching Exercise

1. o	8. d
2. j	9. c
3. i	10. k
4. b	11. s
5. g	12. h
6. l	13. f
7. e	14. q

Answers to Matching Exercise (continued)

15. r	18. n
16. p	19. m
17. a	

Answers to Self-Test

1. b	11. a
2. b	12. c
3. d	13. b
4. d	14. a
5. a	15. d
6. c	16. F
7. c	17. T
8. a	18. F
9. b	19. F
10. c	20. T

CHAPTER 7   Answer Key

Answers to Matching Exercise

1. g	7. e
2. b	8. c
3. k	9. j
4. d	10. h
5. a	11. f
6. i	

Answers to Self-Test

1. c	11. a
2. d	12. d
3. a	13. c
4. a	14. a
5. b	15. b
6. d	16. T
7. b	17. F
8. c	18. F
9. c	19. T
10. b	20. F

CHAPTER 8   Answer Key

Answers to Matching Exercise

1. h	6. j
2. e	7. d
3. c	8. l
4. g	9. f
5. b	10. k

Harcourt Brace & Company.

Answers to Matching Exercise (continued)
11. a   12. i

Answers to Self-Test
1. d   11. a
2. d   12. c
3. c   13. b
4. d   14. c
5. b   15. d
6. a   16. F
7. a   17. T
8. c   18. F
9. b   19. T
10. b   20. F

CHAPTER 9   Answer Key

Answers to Matching Exercise
1. c   5. a
2. f   6. e
3. d   7. b
4. g

Answers to Self-Test
1. b   11. c
2. a   12. b
3. c   13. d
4. d   14. a
5. c   15. a
6. d   16. F
7. a   17. F
8. b   18. T
9. d   19. F
10. c   20. T

CHAPTER 10   Answer Key

Answers to Matching Exercise
1. d   6. a
2. c   7. h
3. i   8. b
4. f   9. e
5. g

Answers to Self-Test
1. c   4. c
2. b   5. b
3. d   6. a

Harcourt Brace & Company.

Answers to Self-Test (continued)

7. c	14. b
8. b	15. d
9. d	16. F
10. a	17. T
11. a	18. F
12. c	19. T
13. d	20. F

CHAPTER 11   Answer Key

Answers to Matching Exercise

1. i	13. q
2. n	14. m
3. g	15. b
4. a	16. u
5. l	17. h
6. j	18. v
7. c	19. w
8. e	20. p
9. o	21. r
10. d	22. f
11. s	23. t
12. x	24. k

Answers to Self-Test

1. d	11. a
2. a	12. a
3. b	13. d
4. b	14. b
5. c	15. c
6. b	16. F
7. a	17. T
8. b	18. F
9. d	19. T
10. c	20. T

CHAPTER 12   Answer Key

Answers to Matching Exercise

1. d	5. h
2. g	6. a
3. b	7. c
4. e	8. f

Answers to Self-Test

1. d	4. a
2. c	5. a
3. b	6. c

Answers to Self-Test (continued)

7. c
8. b
9. c
10. d
11. a
12. a
13. d

14. b
15. b
16. F
17. F
18. T
19. F
20. T

CHAPTER 13 Answer Key

Answers to Matching Exercise

1. e
2. o
3. d
4. l
5. i
6. t
7. g
8. n
9. a
10. p
11. v

12. k
13. s
14. c
15. q
16. b
17. m
18. u
19. h
20. r
21. f
22. j

Answers to Self-Test

1. b
2. d
3. c
4. a
5. b
6. c
7. c
8. a
9. c
10. b

11. d
12. d
13. a
14. b
15. d
16. F
17. T
18. F
19. F
20. F

CHAPTER 14 Answer Key

Answers to Matching Exercise

1. d
2. j
3. f
4. b
5. a
6. h

7. e
8. k
9. c
10. i
11. g

Answers to Self-Test

1. a	11. c
2. c	12. d
3. c	13. c
4. d	14. a
5. b	15. b
6. d	16. F
7. b	17. T
8. c	18. T
9. d	19. F
10. a	20. T

CHAPTER 15 Answer Key

Answers to Matching Exercise

1. e	6. b
2. f	7. i
3. a	8. c
4. h	9. g
5. d	

Answers to Self-Test

1. b	11. d
2. a	12. b
3. a	13. c
4. c	14. c
5. d	15. a
6. d	16. T
7. d	17. F
8. c	18. T
9. a	19. F
10. b	20. F

CHAPTER 16 Answer Key

Answers to Matching Exercise

1. g	6. a
2. b	7. c
3. e	8. d
4. i	9. h
5. f	

Answers to Self-Test

1. c	7. a
2. c	8. b
3. d	9. d
4. b	10. d
5. a	11. c
6. c	12. b

Harcourt Brace & Company.

Answers to Self-Test (continued)

13. b	17. F
14. a	18. F
15. d	19. T
16. T	20. F

CHAPTER 17   Answer Key

Answers to Matching Exercise

1. o	9. j
2. e	10. m
3. i	11. k
4. b	12. c
5. p	13. h
6. d	14. n
7. g	15. f
8. a	16. l

Answers to Self-Test

1. d	11. d
2. b	12. c
3. a	13. b
4. c	14. b
5. c	15. c
6. b	16. F
7. a	17. T
8. c	18. T
9. d	19. F
10. b	20. T

CHAPTER 18   Answer Key

Answers to Matching Exercise

1. e	4. f
2. b	5. a
3. d	6. c

Answers to Self-Test

1. b	11. c
2. d	12. a
3. b	13. c
4. b	14. d
5. a	15. d
6. d	16. T
7. c	17. F
8. c	18. T
9. b	19. F
10. a	20. F

CHAPTER 19   Answer Key

Answers to Matching Exercise

1. e	6. c
2. b	7. f
3. i	8. a
4. g	9. h
5. j	10. d

Answers to Self-Test

1. b	11. a
2. a	12. d
3. c	13. a
4. b	14. b
5. a	15. d
6. d	16. F
7. c	17. T
8. c	18. F
9. b	19. F
10. d	20. T

CHAPTER 20   Answer Key

Answers to Matching Exercise

1. j	12. k
2. l	13. o
3. q	14. p
4. b	15. a
5. n	16. u
6. s	17. h
7. e	18. f
8. c	19. m
9. t	20. d
10. g	21. r
11. i	

Answers to Self-Test

1. d	11. d
2. b	12. b
3. b	13. c
4. a	14. a
5. d	15. d
6. d	16. T
7. b	17. F
8. c	18. T
9. a	19. F
10. d	20. T

Harcourt Brace & Company.

CHAPTER 21   Answer Key

Answers to Matching Exercise

1. e
2. b
3. f

4. a
5. d
6. c

Answers to Self-Test

1. b
2. c
3. d
4. a
5. d
6. c
7. b
8. a
9. c
10. b

11. a
12. c
13. d
14. d
15. c
16. T
17. F
18. T
19. T
20. F

Harcourt Brace & Company.